D0199867

THE
CHAMPIONS'
GAME

A TRUE STORY

SAUL RAMIREZ

as told to JOHN SEIDLITZ

Published by Canter Press
P.O. Box 167607
Irving, TX, 75061
www.canterpress.com

Copyright © 2017 Canter Press, All rights reserved.

No part of this book may be reproduced in any form or by electronic or
mechanical means, including photocopy, recording, scanning, or other,
without prior permission from the publisher, except for the use of brief
quotations in a book review.

To obtain permission to use material from this work, please submit a
written request to Canter Press Permissions Department,
P.O. Box 167607, Irving, TX, 75061

For related titles and support materials visit www.canterpress.com.

ISBN 978-0-9977402-3-3
ISBN 978-0-9977402-4-0 (hc)

4.17

DEDICATION

This book is dedicated to all team members of the Henderson Chess Club, past, present and future:

No matter where you find yourselves on the board of life, may you be mastering the game as the champions you were taught to be.

TABLE OF CONTENTS

INTRODUCTION

> *Fronterizos, people who live on the border, are unclassifiable hybrids. They are not exactly immigrants. Immigrants don't cross back and forth as much. Border crossers are a people on the margin. ...But I think the trend is changing. ...Their story, or should I say, our story is increasingly becoming a part of the mainstream.*"
>
> – David Dorado Romo
> *Ringside Seat to a Revolution*

On a pristine day, standing on the ridge of the Franklin Mountains that ring the town of El Paso, Texas, one can see far into the vast expanse of northern Mexico. In fact, El Paso is more of a suburb of a Mexican city nearly twice as large, just a coyote's howl across the border: Ciudad Juárez, world-renowned as one of the most violent towns on the planet and home to one of the most notorious drug cartels in the Americas.

By contrast, if you want to live in a clean, safe city, you can't do much better than El Paso. It's a hidden gem. People there are smart, educated, and polite. There's virtually no gang graffiti visible anywhere. Neighborhoods, even the poorer ones, are well kept and clean. A good portion of the credit for all that goes to the importance the Latino culture places on family. People genuinely care about one another in El Paso. They want to help each other. They treat each other with respect. They'll give you whatever they have. It's called *ganas*: to give your all.

In El Paso there is a certain magical quality, a confident excellence emanating from this ruggedly beautiful town in the dusty desert surrounded by mountains cleaved in two by the mighty Rio Grande. The great river slithers through the city like a vibrant green serpent, providing life and stealing dreams—depending on which side you're on.

Some of this magical quality resides in El Paso's Henderson Middle School, where the atmosphere is relaxed, the students are cheerful, and the campus is clean and orderly. As it should be. All of the students at this school qualify for the free lunch program (and depend on it). The school has been visited by top officials (judges, mayors, and other dignitaries) due, in part, to the efforts of Saul Ramirez, a 30-year-old dad and husband who teaches art at Henderson during the day and coaches the chess team after school. Yet, the excellence is not so much the chess that Ramirez teaches (even though he's a former Texas state chess champion), but what he is doing with these underprivileged students. He is showing them how to achieve lofty intellectual goals the kids themselves could only dream they might one day accomplish. This is because Ramirez possesses a singular ability to use chess to expand the minds, the insight, and even the future possibilities of the sixth, seventh and eighth grade students he teaches.

For example, *visualization, foresight, critical thinking,* and *strategic planning* are not terms that usually come to mind when thinking of at-risk 11-, 12- and 13-year-old children barely out of elementary school. Kids on the border don't generally spend time thinking about concepts like *guard your queen, control your center,* and *protect your king.* For these kids, hazy dreams of beating highly privileged students from "fancy" schools in upper-crust neighborhoods aren't on the radar. They have bigger issues to deal with in life. Which is why it borders on the miraculous that middle schoolers whose lives are riddled with hardship and trials choose to voluntarily—even *enthusiastically*—commit countless hours every week to the practice of a game that, less than two years earlier, they had known virtually nothing about.

But Ramirez intertwines life principles with rules from the game of chess to produce winners. And winning is something these kids want. Under his caring but firm tutelage, the students hunker down, deal with the daily challenges of life, shrug off troubling national news riddled with racism and division, and instead trust Ramirez to mentor them in their new extra-curricular passion—chess.

To make it to the national competition, the Henderson kids would have to topple dozens of state teams and prove to detractors and opponents alike that no obstacle, no matter how daunting, can suppress the resilience and spirit of children who dare to dream.

But could they even compete statewide, much less nationally? Could they beat kids from private college prep schools? Could they take on New York teams that had scores of players and a dozen chaperones? Could twelve middle school kids from one of the poorest zip codes in America, kids who had precious little to their names *but* their good names, scrape enough money together to afford travel to McAllen, Texas, or Louisville, Kentucky?

In the end, the outcome really didn't matter all that much. Their minds and lives had already been altered beyond their wildest dreams.

A revolution is taking place in El Paso. A revolution of the *mind*, led by a brilliant young educator named Saul Ramirez. What he is doing in the lives of the children he is tasked with teaching is artful genius. It is astonishing. It is beautiful.

GO BIG or GO HOME

> *The chessboard is the world, the pieces are the phenomena of the universe, the rules of the game are what we call the laws of Nature. The player on the other side is hidden from us. We know that his play is always fair, and patient."*
>
> - T.H. Huxley, *A Liberal Education*

Oh God! I thought. *It's happening all over again.* It was like a bad movie. Worse. It was a nightmare. The traffic wasn't budging. I was like a man trying to smile in front of a firing squad.

My cell phone rang. It was Mr. Herrera, in the van in front of me.

"What do we do, bro?" he said, his voice a mixture of amusement and worry.

I glanced in the rearview mirror. The kids in my van were starting to clamor about being late to their first nationals.

I said, "Dude, there's so much traffic...we're going to have to..."

"Bro, we need to get there."

"I know that, Adrian."

If you get to the nationals late, they don't care. If you arrive twenty minutes after the round, you lose the round, period. Plain and simple. No show, no go. And it tumbles like dominos from there, with one forfeiture following another, depending on how fast the games go and how much later you arrive.

I saw a sign up ahead that said DO NOT ENTER - EMERGENCY LANES ONLY.

As a chess champion, player and coach, I don't recommend the course of action we were about to take. But, man, sometimes you gotta pivot!

Go big or go home!

I watched as Mr. Herrera's van suddenly shot into the emergency lane.

I muttered to myself, "I don't know where this guy's going, but..."

I hit the gas and stayed on his tail.

RULE 1: Go Big or Go Home

The kids started whooping, "Come on, Mister! We gotta get there first!"

May as well have been the Indy 500. It was crazy. I don't know how we did it, but we got there on time. We skidded into the 2015 National Chess Championship. We arrived in style.

In chess, that most ancient of games, you must make the most of chances that come your way. Always be on the lookout for opportunities that present themselves for you to improve your position on the board (and isn't life our board?).

In Mexico there is a saying that goes, *"Come cuando hay"* (Eat while it's there). The English equivalent is, "Strike while the iron's hot." But I say it like this: Go big or go home! It's one of the first rules I teach my students. When you spot an opportunity, grab it and run. It could be your pathway to checkmate on the board of your life.

Let me give you an example. It's about a girl. Her name is Edna.

It was our senior year; we were both in sports. She was in volleyball, I was in wrestling, and we had practice around the same time.

One day after practice, I was hanging out by the gym, and she came out and caught my eye. I went up to her and we started talking. Time flew and it started to get kind of late. She lived a few blocks away so I decided to walk her home.

Being a gentleman, I took her backpack and carried it for her.

The Champions' Game

Back then I had a friend named Ignacio Flores, or Nacho, as we all liked to call him. He was my best friend. We'd always be together, side by side. He, too, was a chess player at Bowie High School. Actually, he was probably one of the best chess players that I knew here in El Paso.

He was a tall guy and also a very challenging human being. To be honest, sometimes he was a little too smart. He grew up in Segundo Barrio, the same place that I grew up. We were together in both the chess world and the real world.

The day I was walking Edna home for the first time, Nacho was walking with us. I kept telling him to leave, which proved to be quite a challenge. The funny thing about Nacho was he didn't know how to take a hint. I knew, though, that he was always hungry. I had a plan.

"Hey Nacho, go get yourself a burger."

"Nah, I wanna go with you guys."

He wasn't taking the hint. I tried again.

"No, why don't you go get yourself a burger?"

"Nah, I'm good."

"Nacho, go get a burger!"

I even gave him money to go buy himself a burger. And he just didn't want to go! I had to make myself more clear.

"Hey. Just go get yourself a burger, I need some alone time, a'ight!"

RULE 1: Go Big or Go Home

After what seemed like an eternity, he finally got the hint. He went to Whataburger, which was right by Edna's house, and he let me walk her home by myself.

Apparently, Nacho was one taco short of a combo plate!

When we got to her house, we stopped and stood at the corner, talking. This was my moment: Go big or go home! I leaned in and gave her a kiss. This was my way of asking her to be my girlfriend.

As for Nacho, over time we kind of separated as friends. He went his way and I went mine. As for Edna, she became my wife. Sometimes, when you spot an opportunity and run with it, it can change your life.

Here's another example. In May of 2010, I was 24 years old, I didn't have a job, and I had heard about an open teaching position at Henderson Middle School. Other than my wife and our six-year-old son Saulito and two-year-old daughter Frida, I had nothing at that time. *Nada.* Zip. No job, no money. For the longest time, I had been working toward becoming a teacher. I was ready. This was my chance.

I took a shower, grabbed my admittedly thin résumé, and headed for the door.

"Where are you going, *mi amor*?" my beautiful Edna asked me.

> *nada* – nothing
> *mi amor* – my love ✳

"Job interview. At Henderson."

"Really? How many other interviews do you have lined up?"

"I only need one, *querida*," I said.

I kissed her goodbye and hurried out. I needed a haircut before I presented myself to Henderson Middle School.

When I arrived at the school office, I told the receptionist that I was there to submit my résumé. She held out her hand and I handed it to her. She glanced at it, probably to make sure I had the basics covered. Contact info, education, experience, extra-curricular activities. It was only one page long. Other than a few tutoring and volunteering jobs and an internship, I didn't have a lot of applicable experience.

As she was reading, she looked up suddenly and said, "You know Gaspar Enríquez?"

"Yes. I know Mr. Enríquez. He was my art teacher at Bowie High School, and now a close friend."

I had put my former art teacher's name on my résumé because he's a very well-known Chicano artist in the southwestern United States. He creates huge scale paintings of gangsters, *cholos*, iconic figures and other colorful, tough characters of grit and substance. No mere muralist, Gaspar paints major, famous works.

She motioned toward a chair in front of the desk and said, "You may sit down."

querida – **beloved**	
cholos – **homies**	✱

RULE 1: Go Big or Go Home

I sat, hoping I would get a chance to speak with the principal. I've never been big on chitchat. I speak carefully, and I'm not overly expressive. Whether speaking English or Spanish, I try to get right to the point.

"I'm Elizabeth Maldonado," said the woman I *thought* was the receptionist, holding out her hand. "I'm the principal here at Henderson."

"El gusto es mío," I said as we shook hands.

Talk about a blessing from *Dios!* I was sitting right in front of the decision-maker herself.

"Do you happen to have a letter of recommendation from Mr. Enríquez?"

"I can get one. I know him personally."

Opportunity was knocking. I told her I would get a letter from Gaspar and she asked me to prepare my portfolio and get it to her, then she would contact me to schedule a formal interview.

I had to strike while the iron was hot. And trust me, jobs that are just a rock's throw from the Mexican border weren't exactly easy to find at that time. Especially not in El Paso (which is so close to Juárez you've got one foot in Mexico).

Many of the 700+ students at Henderson Middle School come and go from Juárez, where they live. They have *tías y tíos* in El Paso, and their moms and dads

el gusto es mío – the pleasure is mine

Dios – God

tías y tíos – aunts and uncles

live just across the border. These children see their parents only on weekends. Their parents send them to school in El Paso because they believe that an education in the U.S. is the best opportunity to improve their children's lives. In Mexico, it is common for citizens to pay for their education after sixth grade. Primary school *(primaria)* education is free. But often, families have to pay for middle school *(secundaria)* and high school *(prepa)*. Needless to say, few children of impoverished families can afford to pay to go to school after they turn 12. So they go to work.

Talk about challenges. But challenges were nothing new to me. I grew up on challenges. I was going to get this job at Henderson. I had a plan.

Before I reached my car outside in the early summer heat of the Henderson parking lot, I had already put together a mental list of other people I should get letters of recommendation from, important people who had mentored me when I was young, people who were responsible for getting me prepared to be able to take advantage of opportunities. People like author and historian David Dorado Romo.

I first met David Romo in the summer of 1996 when I was ten years old, between fifth and sixth grade.

Though he was a history teacher back then, I'd heard that he was starting a summer school chess club at the elementary school I would be attending. I

mejor que nada –
better than nothing ✳

knew nothing about chess back then, but I didn't have anything else to do and it was better than being at home. *Mejor que nada...*

My home consisted of three rooms: a kitchen, a living room (if you want to call it that) where all five family members slept, and a bathroom. I didn't have space to read, no place to chill on a hot summer day, no privacy at all. So of course I wanted to play chess. Whatever that was.

When I arrived at school that day, there were a few other kids waiting to hear about the summer program.

Mr. Romo brought out a black t-shirt that had Segundo Barrio Chess Club emblazoned across the chest. "Who wants a shirt like this?" he said.

It was *bien padre*—very cool!

I was from Segundo Barrio, the roughest ghetto in all of El Paso in the poorest zip code in the nation, the famous 79901. Free Segundo shirt? Oh yeah, I'm in.

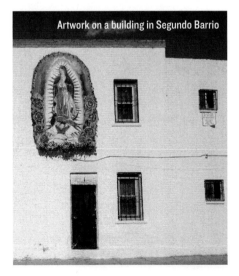
Artwork on a building in Segundo Barrio

My hand shot up. "I want a shirt like that," I said.

Then came the catch.

"Okay. But you gotta stay the whole summer."

The Champions' Game

I was proud of Segundo Barrio. So I could tough it out for a few weeks to get a cool shirt like that. It beat hanging out at home. So I learned how to play chess...for that shirt.

My first chess tournament, as an almost-sixth grader, was against a kindergartner. He was half my age. And the kid destroyed me. He beat me like my mama beating a rug on the clothesline out in back of our little apartment. It was merciless.

I was okay with it, though, because I was playing for the shirt. And one of the things Mr. Romo had taught us early on in those summer weeks was focus, so you can keep track of why you're making the moves you're making—on the chessboard and in life. So I hung in there and kept learning whatever Mr. Romo taught.

Por la camisa became my mantra.

But he was getting chess in my mind, too.

Sure enough, at the beginning of the school year, Mr. Romo gave us shirts. Only they were gray, they said Roosevelt across the chest, and they had yellow letters. Say whaaat? They were the suckiest shirts I had ever laid my eyes on.

"Mr. Romo," I told him, "you promised us Segundo Barrio shirts. I want my shirt to say Segundo Barrio."

That's what I wanted. That's what I joined the club for. That's why I was learning to play chess. I wanted my Segundo Barrio shirt.

"I'm sorry, Saul, I had to work with Roosevelt," he explained lamely.

por la camisa – **for the shirt**

✳

RULE 1: Go Big or Go Home

"Really, Mr. Romo? You're going with that story to give us this?"

"They're not going to allow us to put Segundo Barrio on black shirts with yellow lettering."

Too controversial, I guess. Like Compton. Or South Central. Or 8 Mile. Only cooler, because my neighborhood was different. I was proud of my 'hood. I wanted to put Segundo on the map so everyone else would be proud of it, too.

I just had to figure out how.

As far as chess, I stuck with it and I stuck with David Romo. I liked the guy. He was cool. He was fun. He knew everything about everything. He came from a prominent, solid El Paso family. He had a degree from Stanford. He knew chess. He taught us everything.

In those early days playing chess in sixth grade, he took us everywhere to compete, often paying most of the costs himself. We stayed up to ten kids in a room. But he was giving us very important lessons, giving us books to study, teaching us the basics about life through chess. Back then, as an elementary kid from the barrio, I didn't know anything about college or scholarships or school beyond high school. But he kept pouring it all into me. Chess and life. Life and chess.

Now, many years later, I had David Romo to thank. He not only taught me how to play chess, but gave me the tools to put together a great life for myself. The biggest lesson I learned from David Romo? Never quit! No matter what, never give up in life.

It was a lesson that applied to chess, too. Even if you're lagging behind or facing a challenging opponent, don't quit, because you never know what's just ahead that could improve your position. It was a lesson I would soon be teaching my students.

David Romo, now a published author, wasn't my only inspiration. My art teachers, Gaspar Enríquez and Mauricio Olague, were also big influences in my life. They mentored me, taught me, coached me. They inspired me to go to college and earn my degree. Was it possible that recommendations from men like these could help me gain an advantage in the job I was hoping to land at Henderson? I sure hoped so. All I could do was try.

When I told David Romo about the job opportunity at Henderson, he immediately agreed to write me a letter of recommendation.

I then contacted Mr. Olague, from Bowie High School. When I told him I had an interview, he suggested I do a pre-interview with him at his house to prepare me for my talk with Mrs. Maldonado. It was like putting a top-notch dream team together to ensure my victory.

Mr. Olague said, "You have to be more prepared than anyone else for that interview."

He also put me through my paces. We went over everything the school would need. We pored over the STAAR (the State of Texas Assessment of Academic Readiness) program reports and went through all the scores. We discussed how art could help increase students' scores. We went over every single aspect of art. We even put together a detailed lesson planner as to what I would propose to teach the students every single day for the entire school year. Mr. Olague taught me: the art of teaching, how to behave in school environments, how principals think and what they expected from teachers. It was grueling and invaluable at the same time.

During the process of preparing for my interview with Mrs. Maldonado, I discovered another candidate for the job was currently completing an internship at Henderson. That gave her an inside track. Plus, she was a polished young woman who had graduated from a prestigious college. It was a real blow to me and it got inside my head (something you never want an opponent to do to you in chess).

"This girl is already at Henderson," I told Mr. Olague. "She's doing her internship there. She's going to get the job."

"Well, you will certainly be going to your interview well prepared," he responded.

The advice of David Romo resounded in my head. Never quit!

I pushed away the doubt and submitted my freshly polished résumé and the letters of recommendation to Mrs. Maldonado. She scheduled an interview.

It was in God's hands now. I had done all I could.

A couple of weeks earlier, my mother wanted to know what I was going to do now that I had almost earned my degree from UTEP (University of Texas El Paso).

"Let me lay it out for you, Mamá," I replied. "Here's what I'm going to do: I'm going to graduate. I'm going to go to Las Vegas with my wife for a little vacation. We're going to have fun. And I'm going to come back and I'm going to have one interview. And I'm going to get the job."

"What interview? What job, *mijo*?"

"I don't know, Mamá. But it will happen. You'll see."

I told my wife the same. But I added one other thing. Orange. I didn't know why. "Something about orange," I said. Orange has always been a very calming color to me, and in my thoughts about my future, I saw orange.

"But you haven't had any interviews," my wife said, ignoring the orange part. "What are you going to do? There are no jobs anywhere."

"It's going to come. I only need one opportunity. One interview. Just watch."

In life, as in chess, you have to move with confidence.

So, we went to Vegas. And three weeks later I heard about the job opening at Henderson. It was on!

When I arrived, I saw the other candidate finishing her interview. She was poised, well dressed, and had a leather portfolio that was adorned with acrylics and expensive paints.

I was in trouble.

As I stood to go into Mrs. Maldonado's office holding my worn, white binder notebook with the scuffed plastic sheet protectors containing my

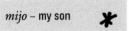

mijo – my son

portfolio, I wondered how the other candidate had done. Did she represent the type of kids who attended Henderson? Did she believe in the kids and have their best interests at heart? She probably did. After all, she had won an internship there.

Mrs. Elizabeth Maldonado was a friendly, attractive woman in her early 40s, with wise, knowing eyes and a no-nonsense demeanor. She kind of resembled an older version of Salma Hayek.

In spite of my intense preparation, I felt decidedly unpolished in comparison to her first interviewee. My presentation was not fancy. My portfolio was narrow in theme and focus.

No! I had to put a stop to that kind of thinking. My portfolio was good. The samples of my work displayed my talent and showed *mi corazón*.

I am already a pretty focused guy, somewhat reserved, and always polite and respectful. But to be honest, I do look a little like a *cholo* from Segundo Barrio. Tall, thickset, with close-cropped dark hair and brown eyes. At first glance in a dark alley at nighttime, sure, you might quicken your pace in the opposite direction.

I stepped into her office and put on the friendliest face I could muster at that moment.

During our preliminary chitchat, Mrs. Maldonado read my letters of recommendation. She noted that like Gaspar Enríquez's wife, she was from San Elizario, just thirty minutes to the south. I showed her a commissioned painting I had been involved

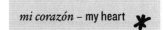

mi corazón – my heart

in making with Gaspar Enriquez for the comedian and actor Cheech Marin. She was impressed.

I was off to a good start.

When the time came to review my portfolio, Mrs. Maldonado took it and turned each page as I carefully explained the drawings, paintings, and photos. I had charcoals, I had paintings, I had sculptures.

She stopped at a painting of my wife. Everybody has that reaction when they see Edna.

"Who is this?"

"This...is my wife." I could not help the note of pride in my voice.

"Why do you have her here?"

"Because she's very important to me. She's my backbone. She's my queen." Like in the game of chess. The queen, the most powerful piece on the board.

"And who is this?"

"This...is my son," I said.

"And this?"

"*Mi tío.*" And so on...The pattern was unmistakable.

"You only do artwork that features your family members?"

"Mostly, yes."

RULE 1: Go Big or Go Home

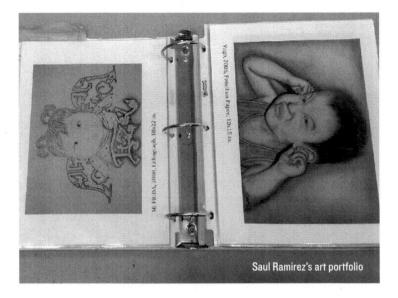

Saul Ramirez's art portfolio

"Why is that?"

"*Mi familia*. My family is the reason I'm doing all of this. That's what drives me. This is the reason I went to school."

Then I put out the lesson planner containing my proposed lesson plans for the year.

I knew that the candidate who preceded me, the woman with the beautiful portfolio cover, had an advantage over me because she was already interning at Henderson. I was sure there were other candidates as well. I also knew that my little white notebook with my drawings, photos, and paintings was a far cry from what the others may have had. But this was me. I was Segundo, and no longer needed a t-shirt to prove it. I was not rich, not by any stretch of the imagination...but neither were the students at Henderson. All I could do was be me and do my best.

Then she asked me if there was anything else I wanted to add.

I hesitated, and then said, "I'd like to start a chess team here at Henderson if I get the job."

I'm sure that wasn't what she was expecting to hear. But I had already given her all the standard interview answers, and now it was time to take the talk in a new direction. To go big. *¿Y por qué no?* Nothing to lose, right?

She looked at me as if I had just said I wanted to start a knitting club. My first impression was that chess wasn't that important to her. Chess is not important to most people. But, I not only loved chess, I was a living example of what it could do in the life of a child.

In my portfolio, I had a photo of me with the Guillen Middle School chess team. I had tutored them when I was in high school, and had coached the team to a win in the Texas state championship, novice division. The picture showed the grinning students with their prize trophy.

As she looked at the photo, Mrs. Maldonado said, "Guillen won first place in chess?"

Guillen happened to be the chief rival of Henderson Middle School in athletics and scholastic activities. I knew that, of course. I had not come to this interview unprepared.

¿Y por qué no? – and why not? ✳

RULE 1: Go Big or Go Home

"Yes. I trained them. And I can do it at Henderson, too."

"Tell me about Guillen."

Guillen Middle School chess team

I told her about how when I was at UTEP working on my Fine Arts degree, I had been a volunteer at Guillen, helping the chess team. The coach had asked me if I'd like to work there as a tutor. I said yes. I trained the team. And they ended up winning a state championship.

"In the entire state?"

"Yes, ma'am."

"And you coached them?"

"Yes, ma'am."

She asked me, "How were you able to do that?"

Now she was on my turf. She was curious about chess. And at chess, I was a champion. This is my game.

I said,

"Because I know what students need at each level.
  I know what the beginner needs.
  I know what the intermediate needs.
  I know what the advanced player needs.
  I know what these children need so they can succeed."

The Champions' Game

"But how are you able to teach these kids to become champions so quickly?"

"The biggest connection is to apply chess to the students' lives so they understand what's going on and they relate the game to their own real-life experiences."

When kids are taught to visualize the rules, they retain those images in their mind and they become life lessons. And once they do that with chess, kids fall in love with the game. And once they've fallen in love with the game, they'll play endless hours. Work at something hard enough and long enough and you will master it.

I told Mrs. Maldonado, "This gets the kids educated and gets them united and working together. That's what a student chess club is all about. The principles of chess are really just rules for life."

Then the principal asked me the final, all-important question. The one I had been waiting for, my checkmate question.

"Tell me, Mr. Ramirez. Why should I hire you for this job? What do you have to offer this school?"

"I will be an awesome art teacher, and I will make state champions out of the Henderson chess team. I did it before. I can do it here."

"You can?"

"Yes."

She looked at me. She smiled.

RULE 1: Go Big or Go Home

She told me she would let me know as soon as she made her decision.

It felt like my entire life was all preparation for that one interview.

In 1996, when I was ten, my dad, who was an accountant, crossed over from Mexico to pick crops in the fields. Later, he got involved with the migrant farm workers as a volunteer social worker, advising and counseling them in the evenings after a long day's work. He would often take me to the fields after school and on weekends, as well as to his social work appointments and meetings, so I could be around the migrant farm workers, help out, and learn. I would give them blankets so they could sleep at the offices and keep warm at night. I would serve them food. We all got to know each other well. I loved the experience.

When I was in elementary school, I was put into the "GT" (gifted and talented) program. But it was difficult for me in the beginning because I mainly spoke Spanish and I struggled with English. Eventually, I was taken out of the program. Maybe it was my lack of fluency in English, since I spent the majority of my time with people who spoke only Spanish. I liked speaking the language of my family and my childhood. Why I was taken out of the gifted and talented program was a mystery to me. But I was just a child, and people didn't tend to explain things to children. Even though they can be very good at figuring things out, my parents were not in the habit of challenging school decisions, like most of the parents in my school.

Sometimes GT programs aren't always about finding kids who are truly gifted, but finding kids who fit a certain mold. I guess I didn't fit the mold. Many of the Spanish-speaking kids I now coach in chess don't fit either. A lot of them also have disabilities that "should" prevent them from being able to master an intellectual game like chess, yet they become champions. It just takes time.

It took me time to become a champion. I started in elementary in Segundo Barrio with David Romo as my coach. After six years of practice, in 2001, I became a state champion. David Romo nurtured that gift in me that just needed time to flourish.

The following year was a year of upheaval and major change. The U.S. sent troops into Afghanistan. I was 16 and was getting involved in social, civil, and political rights activities. I was active in migrant farm worker protests and the student walk-out related to immigrant rights. I was also involved in the movement against tearing down historic buildings in El Paso, and many other worthy causes. We were protesting, closing down streets and doing whatever we needed to do to undo injustices and right wrongs. I loved it. This was my family, *mi gente,* my people.

By then, chess had become much more than just a game to me. Mr. Medina, my high school chess coach and economics teacher, took me to New York City so I could watch the national championship. Chess had allowed me to travel to play in state championships and stay at five-star hotels during high school. Chess was even helping put some extra money in my pockets, because since middle school, I had been regularly crossing the border into Juárez to play the Mexican locals for cash nearly every weekend. Chess was helping me learn all about what was truly important in life. Chess was changing my life.

At the same time, chess was teaching me how to become a champion. The influential men in my young life were teaching me how to behave like one.

Then, the most wonderful, scary thing happened. Something that shouldn't happen to a senior in high school...Edna was pregnant.

We were both 17. We were still in high school. The timing could have been better, but we were in love!

My dad said to me, "You're going to have to get a job."

So I had a meeting with an army recruiter, who encouraged me to serve a tour in the military, earn some money, and then go to college after a few years in the army. But it seemed like a lot of kids my age were going over to Iraq and Afghanistan... and coming back drastically, permanently changed. And not in good ways.

I went to Mr. Medina and asked him what I should do. He didn't think the military was the way to go.

"Go to college," he said. "Whatever it takes to earn your degree, you and Edna are going to go to school. The government system is made for that. You're going to get financial aid and apply for subsidized housing. You're going to get food stamps. You're just going to do it for four years. You're going to go to school and you're both going to graduate. And then you're going to repay everything back to the government."

My high school counselor, Josie Carmona, agreed. She said, "You need to get educated. You need to educate your child, and you need to be ready to make a good life for yourselves. You don't need to join the army to get money for college. If you want money for school, we can help you find financial aid."

She helped Edna and me fill out and file all the necessary paperwork to get financial aid and housing and get into school.

We went to college while we were teenage parents.

When we started school, I told our housing manager, "We're just going to be here for four years."

"Sure," she said. "That's what everybody says."

It was tough. I had no way to get around, so I had to borrow my mom's car. I would wake up at four in the morning to drop her off at work. Sometimes I would walk to school, lugging all my canvases with me to UTEP. It was very difficult. But we persevered, because if we wanted our child to have a decent future, we needed to start building it now, and that meant college degrees for us both.

Sure enough, at the end of my fourth year, when I graduated from UTEP, we went to the subsidy housing manager, handed her our keys, and said, "Here are the keys, ma'am. Thank you."

RULE 1: Go Big or Go Home

And we bought a house. I was 24. With a wife, son, and daughter.

Then we took that trip to Vegas, and I had the interview with Elizabeth Maldonado.

A few days after the interview, Mrs. Maldonado called.

When I hung up Edna said, "Well? Did you get the job?"

I nodded and said, "*Sí, mi amor.* Just like I said I would."

Mrs. Maldonado also gave me a Henderson Middle School t-shirt. The color? Orange.

Now it was time to start planning my next move.

1 — GO BIG OR GO HOME
2 — NO SUCH THING AS LOSING
3 — YOU HAVE TO REALLY WANT IT
4 — DEVELOP YOUR PIECES
5 — PROTECT THE KING
6 — CHERISH YOUR QUEEN
7 — MAKE YOUR MOVES WITH PUR

RULE 2

NO SUCH THING AS LOSING

My first year at Henderson was spent learning my official job as a middle school art teacher and absorbing the "lay of the land" as a professional instructor—all in preparation for my next step: setting up Henderson's first chess team.

In the summer of 2012, two years into my new job, I was settled in enough to begin creating the team. More than 96 percent of Henderson students were from low-income families and a third were English language learners. I knew these kids, they had an amazing spirit. If I could corral that spirit and use it to teach them the rules of chess, I could make them champions. That was the commitment I made to Mrs. Maldonado.

RULE 2: No Such Thing as Losing

I'm an art teacher. I like to recruit with an artistic touch: I see kids who don't know they're chess champions. I have a sort of sixth sense to be able to tell which kids are special. My young cousins, David Alfredo Alvarado and David Ernesto Morales (who we like to affectionately call "the Davids") call me "the chess witch." I can sense how quickly a child will grasp chess and how well they will play the game—even if they have never touched a chess piece before.

I can tell when a student is different, no matter their personal or economic circumstances. And being in El Paso, it was a sure bet that nearly all the kids on the team would come from an economically disadvantaged background. Most of them would have social issues and family challenges. There would be kids who'd been in foster homes, others who were homeless, and even those who had no mother or father in the home and were being raised by an *abuelita* (ah, grandmothers—backbone of the Mexican *familia*!). Some kids would be in special education classes. And others would have loving, intact, well-functioning families.

Greatness is found everywhere.

Since I had already set up and run chess clubs previously, my goal was to have 100 kids join my first Henderson chess team (Go Big, *¿verdad?*). I made a wall poster with blank slots for 100 names. I spent more than a week enticing students with chess talks.

Ten. Students. Joined.

Well...it would just have to be a small team, wouldn't it?

¿verdad? –
true?; isn't that true? ✱

The school didn't have funds for shirts, and we had no money to travel to local or state tournaments, so small would have to be great.

Determined to put a positive spin on it, I smiled and told Edna, "I just slashed the budget by ninety percent!"

One of my rules for the kids to be eligible for the team was that they had to have no lower than a B average. I required them to meet for an hour after school every day for practice, and every Saturday morning for four hours. I gave them a 30-minute lesson on new strategy for practice, followed by 30 minutes of game time. They did homework consisting of puzzles, learning games, and chess history. I hammered the rules and lessons into them every day, over and over.

RULE 2: No Such Thing as Losing

Chess puzzles usually consist of a picture of a chess board with the pieces laid out to represent a point in a game. There are three phases of a chess game: the opening, the middle game, and the end game. The puzzle comes from any of these spots in the game. The kids have to figure out how to "move to mate" in a specific number of moves. The puzzles were designed so that it would be impossible to do so in less than the specified number of moves. Thus, the more moves, the more extended their strategizing, making it a more difficult puzzle.

The core of our work together became puzzles and practice ... LOTS of practice! The team members would practice playing each other. Sometimes they played variations on the game for fun and other times in a competition mindset. That's when it got serious. Of course, one person wins and the other loses. On my team, however, we have a rule: "There's no such thing as losing!"

Now, you might be wondering why I say there is no such thing as losing in the game of chess. Here's why: there's no such thing as losing *as long as you learn from your mistakes*. You see, it's a matter of mindset. If you learn from your mistakes, then you have gained, not lost. Then the next time you encounter the same situation, you won't lose.

It was important that they understood this lesson, since they were children who faced uncertain futures. What I have learned, and what I wanted to pass on to them, is that real winners create their own success—*no hay miel sin hiel* (no pain, no gain).

= 12 POINTS

= 9 POINTS

= 5 POINTS

= 3 POINTS

= 3 POINTS

= 1 POINT

The early lessons were easy for the team to learn because most of them had never played the game. Their minds were fresh, like a clean chalkboard, ready to be filled with new information. For example, each chess piece is worth a certain number of points, so I taught them the numerical values. There were: nine points for the queen, three for each knight, one point for each pawn, twelve for the king, three points for each bishop, five for each rook. They kept track of scores during practice. Calculating points helped them improve in math skills.

They also learned about the value of space on the board. For example, you might be winning on points, but what if you were being attacked and were about to lose some space? You could be winning, you could have all these pieces, but in reality, if you didn't have many places to move to, you were in big trouble. It's like being hemmed in on all sides in a threatening situation and having no place to run or hide.

Things they knew instinctively out on the streets, they could apply on the board. Analyzing space and spatial relationships between the pieces in play helped them improve in strategic planning, critical thinking, evaluating, assessing and pivoting.

RULE 2: No Such Thing as Losing

In the beginning, the kids lost more games than they won, but I told them not to get frustrated.

"You are going to lose a lot of games before you improve," I told them.

If you want to become a better player, you have to lose games!

Since learning from their past mistakes made them better players, the only way they could learn from their past mistakes was to study their past games. I taught them to write down every move of every game they played, to study all of the moves of their past games, and to study games played by other players.

I began learning from my mistakes long ago when I was perfecting my game in Mexico. I used to cross the border bridge and walk the pockmarked streets of Juárez to practice with the chess players when I was in middle school. And let me tell you, those Mexican players were *good!* The experience of losing to those savvy players served me well. Plus, I was able to earn a little extra spending cash when I won.

Juárez is a hardcore industrial city, home to hundreds of *maquiladora* factories that employ workers who slave in sweatshop conditions for a couple of dollars per day in the garment, manufacturing, and assembly industries, making or putting together products for companies around the world.

Between 2008 and 2011, America's economic collapse drastically reduced cross-border traffic, but it was the drug-related violence during that period that kept U.S.-born El Paso

maquiladora –
sweatshop

*

Mexicans from making regular visits to their families in Juárez.

With my weekly pilgrimages across the border to visit family members and to play chess with the older guys when I was a kid, my returns to El Paso came with a feeling of relief that I didn't have to be quite as vigilant and observant of those around me. Still, the rugged old city brought with it a mixture of the warmth of *família* with a dose of adrenaline. There was a constant rush of danger lurking in every dusty sundown shadow as I quickly made my way back home after taking a fistful of *pesos* from the *pachucos* I had beaten at chess in the square.

Though I spent much time in Juárez when I was younger, it was El Paso that was home with Segundo Barrio as its *corazón y sangre*. Mission churches dating back to the 1500s and 1600s still held mass in El Paso. Dirt fields overflowed with kids playing soccer, and couples lounging in parks on Sunday afternoons.

El Paso is one of the safest cities in the Western hemisphere. When you're standing in the square in El Paso, seeing the families and all the street activity of simple everyday life, the city has an aura like no other. Almost as if the town was blessed with a special kiss of protection from the lips of *Dios* Himself.

...But even with this charming scenery, not everything was ideal. No place is perfect. Like all cities, El Paso has its troubles, and those troubles affect everybody's morale. However, just because something isn't perfect doesn't mean we give up or despair. Imperfection isn't a problem.

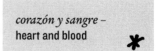

corazón y sangre –
heart and blood

RULE 2: No Such Thing as Losing

You benefit from your mistakes and your losses if you study them and learn from them. I wove this message into my relationship-building with the team. I put the team on a strict regimen of practice, practice, practice: learning from every "loss." I had the novice kids study ten or fifteen chess problems for homework each day; twenty or thirty for my advanced students. Eventually, I had them study two or three games per week. I was tempted to take them to some of the chess clubs across the border in Juárez so they could practice like I used to when I was in middle school. The kids would benefit from that type of exposure.

In the meantime, I had them playing a two-minute speed chess game called Blitz to help them learn how to quickly analyze the board in order to make the right moves under pressure. It was a fun game, but it had a purpose beyond merely playing fast: it taught them to think and to pivot quickly when they had to make the right move right away.

The students learned so many games that they would sometimes get stuck into thinking, "Oh, this happened before in another game, so I know what's gonna happen next." Which isn't always the case. Life is fluid, things change. Not everything ends up the way we think it will just because it happened before. Blitz helped the students avoid that mindset by teaching them how to improvise and not get stuck into a certain track of thinking.

I also had them practice tactics by doing problems that helped them analyze the best possible moves to improve their position on the board. On Saturday mornings, I had them come in from eight until noon and do four one-hour sessions. If they didn't do the work at home (some students also had a volleyball game or football practice or other after-school activity), their chess homework might take an hour and a half. If they wanted to get really good, I told them they would have to do two hours of chess homework in addition to the regular practices.

The main thing was to *play*. Win or lose, just play. I prepped and trained the kids by having them compete against students from other schools at little local tournaments, to get them practicing in competitive environments.

The kids were handling the pressure of constant class work, homework, practice, memorizing, and studying past games like little champs, uncomplaining and determined. I loved it!

By 2013, the team was in good shape and the kids were learning quickly. The time was near for them to take their first big step. The 2013 Texas state championship was scheduled for March, in McAllen. Six of the ten members of the team were going. Things were coming together. All we needed was money for food, van rental, gas, and hotel.

I went to the principal, Mrs. Maldonado. She suggested we do a lock-in fund raiser at Peter Piper Pizza restaurant. So we did— and the community showed up in support of the kids. Between the neighbors, the parents, and the children, we got the small amount of money we needed for the trip to McAllen.

The first-ever Henderson Chess Club team was headed to the 2013 state tournament.

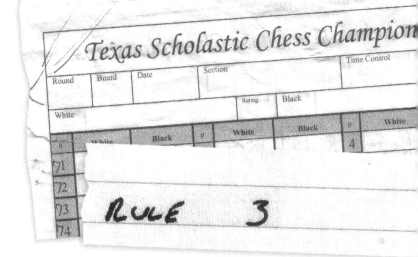

RULE 3

YOU HAVE TO <u>REALLY</u> WANT IT

In preparation to compete at the 2013 Texas Scholastic Chess Championships in the Middle School Novice Division in McAllen, Texas, we raised over $3,000. It was just enough to get six of the team members to the tournament in McAllen. Whether or not they would win was not the issue. It was that they would have an experience they'd never had before and would always remember. One that would inspire them to new heights.

That year, at the Texas Scholastic Championships, undaunted by the fact that most of them had been playing chess for less than two years, the kids on the team fought onward -- even though they were nervous and intimidated by the sea of players at the event.

By the last round, four of them were close enough to the top of the leader-board that they were playing each other. They had beat out nearly every other contestant in the entire state.

Before we had left for McAllen, I had been pretty sure we would place, but I hadn't expected the miracle the team pulled off: they came home as state champs. They had played against 15 of the best teams and 80 of the best players in Texas. It was the team's first state tournament and first state championship. I had held to the promise I'd made to Mrs. Maldonado when she'd hired me as an art teacher at Henderson Middle School: I delivered her a state championship.

The media attention made it even more official, and made the kids and their families proud...

> ## EL PASO'S HENDERSON MIDDLE SCHOOL CHESS TEAM CROWNED KINGS OF TEXAS
>
> Six students from Henderson Middle School showed flashes of brilliance this past weekend, capturing the 2013 Texas Scholastic Chess Tournament championship in McAllen, Texas. ...The Henderson team, made up of seventh- and eighth-graders, placed every one of its players within the top 12 individually. ...Carlos Rios told reporters, 'I was kind of worried and nervous because I was going against my teammate,' said Rios, who played Hernandez. 'And I know how good he is.' ...Ruiz, Rios and Hernandez will move on to high school next year..."
>
> - *The El Paso Times*[1]

[1] *El Paso Times* online, March 26, 2013, in a story by Aaron Bracamontes, titled "El Paso's Henderson Middle Chess Team Crowned Kings of Texas"

RULE 3: You Have to Really Want It

When we got back to El Paso after the win, the kids were so excited that they asked me, "Mister, are we going to nationals?"

The national chess tournament was just a couple of weeks away. There was no way we could get that kind of money together in time.

"I'm sorry guys," I told them. "We can't come up with the money. It's just too much."

Being the champions they were, they responded, "That's fine, mister. We had fun."

The following year, in March of 2014, those who had remained from the 2013 winning team gave the state championship a second try. They won second place and moved up a division. The kids were on fire...okay, maybe not "on fire"—but there were an awful lot of sparks flashing around them!

They also qualified to compete in the 2014 nationals in Atlanta, Georgia. Money was tighter than the previous year, but we got enough cash together to send four players to the nationals.

I told Mrs. Maldonado that I was confident we were going to place in the top five.

So, what happened? Let's just say...nothing went according to plan.

First, we were scheduled to depart on Thursday after school. But the kids were still busy taking their STAAR (State of Texas Assessment of Academic Readiness) exams and we didn't want them to miss a test. But things were running late, so we weren't able to leave on time for the airport.

By the time we finally landed in Atlanta, it was two in the morning. Then, when we got to baggage claim, our luggage wasn't there.

"Ay, *Dios mío*," I muttered. "This is not happening."

Traveling with tired kids at two in the morning is like herding tree sloths. They're groggy, not sure where they are, and can only communicate in grunts and nods.

We eventually found some of our luggage, but not all of it. And the tournament was that same day.

We got to the hotel a couple of hours before dawn. That's when I found out who had clothes and who didn't.

One of the girls' luggage hadn't made it.

"Mister," she said, "I don't have anything to wear tomorrow."

"It's today, *mija*," I yawned.
"Not tomorrow."

The tournament was in just a few hours.

"If I'm gonna play chess, Mister, what do I wear?"

Good question. We drove to Wal-Mart and got her some clothes for the weekend.

...It was not a good start to a national championship competition.

mija –
my daughter ✱

44

RULE 3: You Have to Really Want It

And our problems were just beginning. I began to feel physically ill...even a bit dizzy.

The national competition takes place over a three-day period: Friday, Saturday, and Sunday. After a few hours of sleep, we got the kids up and fed. We made it to the tournament bleary-eyed and wobbly, but on time.

The team from New York had close to 100 kids and 20 or 30 chaperones. They were all decked out in black shirts with yellow stripes. Their team took up the entire middle section of the competition room. That was a lot of brainpower to throw against my four kids.

Friday did not go well.

We had rushed from school to airport to hotel.

We had less than three hours of sleep.

The tournament started a few hours after we arrived.

How did we do?

We won two rounds.
We lost two rounds.
Mathematically, that was not good news.
50%.
 F.

Saturday, we came up a little bit more.

And Sunday, it was over.

The Champions' Game

It seemed like every win that was announced was for "New York!" They had a lot of screaming, cheering kids on that team.

It was all, "And the winner is...New York!"

New York!

New York!

By the time the very last section, the unrated one, was announced, I already knew it was a blowout.

"And last, and unrated, Henderson Middle School." They announced it like an apology.

Sorry, Henderson!

We ended up in nineteenth place.

It was a disaster—especially after we had taken Second Place in state just a couple of weeks earlier. The kids were depressed. I was depressed. I thought I had prepped this team for back-to-back wins, state and nationals.

How did that happen?

When we got back to El Paso, I told Mrs. Maldonado we lost.

"We got nineteenth place," I said.

"That's great!" she said, as if she was wearing earplugs. "You guys did good!"

"No. Nineteenth is *not* good. We wanted at least third."

It hit me hard, really put me down in the dumps. I had been

doing this for so long. And yet, this loss was affecting me so much that I wanted to quit coaching chess altogether.

Edna did not understand why I was so down. She said, "Well, let's figure it out, *mi amor*. What are you getting out of this? What's the purpose? Or are you worried about the cost, the money or—"

"No, it's not money. If I wanted more money, I would've become an engineer or a surgeon or an architect. I'm not looking for money. I'm looking to help kids. It's about the children."

"Well, you are helping the kids. So, why is this loss affecting you so badly?"

I flashed back to eight years earlier, to 2006, when I had been a tutor in college and had put together a little team called Segundo Barrio Chess Club. It had consisted of my two cousins (the Davids), my brother-in-law, my niece and a couple of other kids. And they had won at state.

After the win, I had told the team, "We're gonna win nationals, too."

But we hadn't won then either. The team had gotten crushed, earning twentieth place at the 2006 nationals. It had been another disaster.

At that time, Edna had been pregnant with our daughter,

Frida. After the loss, she was driving us home while I was running things over in my mind, trying to figure out how and where I had gone so wrong at that tournament that we ended up losing badly. I was obsessed with figuring it out, just like this 2014 loss.

Edna had been going the speed limit, about sixty miles per hour, when all of a sudden two of the tires on the van came loose and we were violently slammed to the curb. The van swerved viciously and ended up in the middle of the road.

We thought we were going to die. Our hearts were pounding like jackhammers. We were breathing fast. Our eyes were as wide as dinner plates.

After we realized we had just barely managed to escape with our lives, I told Edna, "Okay, that's it. I'm done. I'm not doing this anymore. No more chess clubs."

Now, eight years later, my 2014 Henderson team had won at state and lost badly at the nationals. I began to wonder if my losing at nationals was an omen. Was something bad going to happen this time, too? Why had I gotten sick at the nationals this time? I never get sick. Was something trying to tell me to get out, to stop coaching chess or stop at the state level?

Maybe I was overreacting. Maybe I had to look at it differently. After all, I had only been in one car accident in my life and that one wasn't my fault. Maybe I had to just remember to live life like I played chess. In life, the streets are like a chessboard. You maneuver through the roads the same way you play a game of chess. You have pieces, like bishops and rooks, coming out in

RULE 3: You Have to Really Want It

every direction. You could be driving straight, knowing where you're going, minding your game, and all of a sudden, a queen comes out of nowhere like a pedestrian off of a curb. You just have to watch out for what's coming at you.

You deal with it.

You keep your eyes open.

You expect the unexpected and handle it without losing your cool.

Still, I didn't know what to do. Keep going? Quit?

What did I really want?

This was a hard question to answer because none of the members of the chess team were staying. They were all going to high school. I would have to start all over again.

It was a sad feeling. I had become so attached to the students. Knowing what made them happy, what made them sad. What made them who they were. They had become almost like my own kids.

Self-doubt crept in. After the second time in a row failing at the nationals, I thought,

Maybe this isn't meant to be.
Maybe I'm not a good coach.
Maybe I'm just not doing it right.

Besides, it was taking up a lot of my free time, every day after school, every weekend. Traveling and playing at local tournaments took from eight in the morning to at least three or four in the afternoon. Another challenge was getting money together to take them to state, then to nationals. It took a lot of time, effort, and emotion. It took time away from my wife and my own children.

"I think I'm done," I told Edna.

"Don't get disappointed, Saul. You're going to get some new kids and they're going to be great. But don't quit."

I didn't know what to do.

I decided I would test the waters for one last try at coaching a team at Henderson and put together a chess camp during summer break of 2014. Then I would decide if I was going to hang it up.

As I was running the summer 2014 chess camp, I found some potential in the kids who showed up. They needed some work, but they showed promise and had heart and desire. Maybe I could make them into something when the new school year started. It would all depend on if the students really wanted to do it, to take it beyond just a cool summer experience, to dig deep, and to come out as champions.

They had to really *want* it.

I had to really *want* it.

RULE 3: You Have to Really Want It

I decided to give it a try. I thought, I'll see if these kids really want to fight for it.

I also had to decide if I really wanted to fight for it.

Then came the moment of truth for me. There was going to be a local tournament.

My summer kids said, "Mister, we're going to the tournament, right?"

"No. Not this weekend, guys. I have plans."

They pushed.

I resisted. They had to want it—really want it.

"Really, Mister? We're not going?"

"Yeah. Sorry guys. You're not quite ready. Besides, I have a family. I have plans."

"Come on, Mister! Let's go!"

"We'll go for the next one. There are tournaments almost every week."

I got home, and my own kids, who were attending MacArthur Elementary summer program, were wearing chess shirts—from their school!

"Dad!" they said the minute I walked in the door. "Look what they gave us at school!"

The Champions' Game

It was a red, neon flag in front of a prize bull.

"A chess shirt? They gave you a chess shirt?"

"Yeah! They know you're the chess coach from Henderson and they know you won state so they gave us shirts!"

"Really."

"Yeah! They're cool, aren't they!?"

"Uh-huh, sure. So, are you joining or you just got shirts?"

"No, no—we're part of the team!"

Okay, that was it. It was like a middleweight boxing champion's girlfriend telling him she met some Joe at the gym who invited her to come see him work out.

"So, uh...you guys are going to the tournament on Saturday?"

"Yeah!"

That was on Thursday.

On Friday, I told the Henderson summer team, "Guys, we're going to the tournament at Wiggs this weekend."

"But Mister...we thought you said we aren't ready."

"We're not. We're gonna get destroyed. I'm telling you right now, we're gonna go, they're gonna murder us, we're gonna get killed. It's not gonna be nice. Don't cry. Just play."

"Alright, Mister!"

RULE 3: You Have to Really Want It

"We're gonna get clobbered. I just want you to know how bad it's gonna be, guys. All of you are new. Those kids have been playing for awhile. A year or two. We're gonna get destroyed. Please don't cry. Just do your best and have fun. Okay?"

"It's alright Mister, we'll have fun!"

Alright, sure, whatever. But it always happened. At every tournament, somebody cries. Whether it was a little kid from elementary or a big kid from high school or a coach. Somebody always cried.

So, sure enough, we showed up to the tournament, and sure enough, we got slapped around, *bad.* We got rung like the Liberty Bell on the 4th of July.

But the kids had *fun!*

And that's when I got it. They were enjoying themselves! It wasn't about winning. They were enjoying every single round. They were enjoying playing the game. They were enjoying being there with each other and with other kids. They were enjoying being with me. My two kids were enjoying it.

During the tournament, my wife said to me, "It seems to me like you may be having a little fun with these kids."

That was the key, right there. *We had fun.* And we ended up only getting third place, but the kids had a blast.

You might be wondering, how is third place fun?

When the kids got third place, they reacted like they had just beaten Boris Spassky, a Grand Master of chess. They were yelling, "Go Henderson!". They got a certificate in a nice plastic frame. They took photos with it like it was pure gold. They mugged for the camera, eyebrows cocked, suave looks on their faces. They were ecstatic.

"But it's only third place," I said.

"It's alright, Mister. *We got something.*"

Another one of the kids told me, "I was kind of planning on getting out. But wow—I just learned this game and we got third? We can actually go places with this chess thing!"

I gave in and decided not to flatten their enthusiasm.

"Well...way to go, guys!"

I never did tell them that at that tournament that day, a grand total of only four teams had been competing. Because to perpetually "last place kids," third place was a huge victory, even if it was third out of four.

As far as I was concerned, I had fun because they had fun. And they redeemed my heart for coaching the game.

It was time to create a winning Henderson Chess Club 2.0.

RULE 4

DEVELOP YOUR PIECES

In chess, you bring out the knights and bishops early because no piece can win the battle all by itself. You can't send the queen out to do all your work and expect her to win alone. You can't send the knight out by himself and think he will capture all the other pieces. You have to bring all of your pieces into the battle. You put what you know into action by moving the right pieces into play: you develop your pieces.

Winning is a team effort.

Having every player on a chess team prepared to win means you will have a deep bench, a strong bench, a bench that can go the distance against any opponent. Chess is a game of endurance. *Así es la vida.*

> *Así es la vida –*
> such is life ✳

The Champions' Game

From day one of the new school year, I was out recruiting new team members to add to my summer crew.

Initially, I found twenty students who wanted to be on the team. That number dwindled down as some dropped out for various reasons. That left a core of a dozen students who seemed eager and determined. But the great majority of them had less than six months of experience playing chess.

I had my work cut out for me. I could only hope the team would rise to the challenge that lay ahead for us all. I was planning to take *this* dynamic dozen all the way to the top...

Pedro "Pedrito" Escobar was an 11-year-old sixth grader who looked like a miniature Elvis Presley. He was a little GQ kid with slick dance moves. He came from a supportive family and had a 14-year-old brother, a 16-year-old sister, and a 20-year-old sister who was living on her own. Pedrito had been in the summer program and his mother was a volunteer at Henderson. He was a real character. He liked to tell "Yo mama" jokes (you know, the kind of jokes like—"Yo mama is so big that when she steps backward, she beeps").

Next was 12-year-old Eduardo Retana, Pedrito's buddy. He liked to be called by his last name. Even when he wrote his name, he always put his last name first. Retana was very quiet, and had a brother and two sisters. His mother worked as a cleaner at a spa, and also worked a full shift at a restaurant. She had only Sundays and Mondays off. Retana's dad lived in Juárez, so Retana would often cross the border to work with him to make money. Retana also came to the team from the summer chess club. He was a kid who carried labels—the kind that bother kids of that age: Special Ed, English language learner, economically disadvantaged. But in Retana's case all you saw was a quiet kid with sweet eyes who was determined to succeed at the champion's game. He was a budding musician who loved *corridos*.

Third was Leo Andres Gonzales, a first-generation American, who, until September of 2014, had never even touched a chess piece. Leo's family lived in El Paso. That fall, his dad brought him in and told me, "Leo wants to play chess." He was 12 when he joined, an only child who enjoyed a comfortable life with very actively involved parents. His dad was an accounting professor at El Paso Community College (I could relate; my dad was an accountant). His mom was a volunteer at Henderson and was always around, helping out. One interesting note, Leo had a pet snake. His mom said the snake was his only friend. He needed the chess team.

Brandon "Classic Man" Caballero was an 11-year-old sixth grader who had been in the summer program and continued onto the team in the fall. He had family in Juárez that he would often visit. He had one brother and parents who

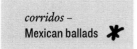

corridos –
Mexican ballads

were very present in his life. The kids on the team called him "Classic Man" because of his clothes. He always looked classy, even though he was economically disadvantaged. The kids weren't picking on him; it was just that he was very stereotypically "Mexican." He also happened to enjoy playing soccer; he loved being on teams. Brandon was not very organized when it came to school. However, in chess, he strategically planned the death of his opponent on the board!

 **Steven Alexis Mejía** was 11 years old when his mom pushed him to join the chess team that fall. At first he was hesitant about spending his afternoons after school learning how to play chess, after all it was his mom who had "encouraged" him to join the team. He struggled at first with the game, but soon became an avid player and a top performer in tournaments. He was friends with my son, Saulito, who had been born around the same time as Steven. He also grew up in our neighborhood. He had a younger sister. His dad was a security guard and his mother was a teacher. Although soft spoken, Steven came across as a natural leader. He has dreams of becoming an architect.

 **Christopher Andrew "Babyface" Carmona** was 12 when he joined the team. He and his 15-year-old brother lived with their grandmother, who had been taking care of him since the day he was born. His parents were not around. He was a diligent student who consistently got good grades, even though he really had to work

hard to achieve them. His life experiences could have hardened him, but when people met him they said he projected a kindness that was hard to forget. When he joined the team that fall as a sixth grader, all he knew of chess was that "it's something you put your toys in, *¿verdad?*"

Thirteen-year-old José Rodrigo Vanegas was in seventh grade and from Juárez, where he often visited family. He, along with his two brothers and two sisters, lived with their mother who was working while finishing school and raising her children. In fact, they had lived in a shelter for awhile. When I heard he was from Juárez, I thought, "This is going to be a good kid." He had been playing chess for two years. And, just as I did when I was his age, he felt more comfortable speaking Spanish than English.

Lirio Amanalli Gomez was a very shy and soft-spoken 12-year-old seventh grader when she joined the team in 2014. At first glance, you would think a strong wind would carry her off, but I discovered a backbone of steel in her as time went on. She was the youngest of three sisters who lived with their mom, who was very involved in their school activities. When she was younger, her father would practice chess with her—mostly just moving pawns around the board. In elementary school she'd been in a chess program. Now she wanted to get a little more serious about it. It brought back bittersweet memories.

The Champions' Game

 **Manuel Esteban "Manny" Tejada** was 12 years old and in sixth grade when he joined the Henderson Chess Club. He had two sisters. His mom and dad worked in the insurance business. He played football and basketball on the city league teams and was very accomplished at both. He was also in the Henderson band. Manny had been taught chess that summer at a different day camp. He enjoyed trying new things and liked that chess was "a gentleman's game." He wanted to learn more, so the first day of school, he joined the team. A gifted and talented student, Manny was a real character and would quickly prove to be the spirit of the team. He had a larger-than-life personality, and his presence filled any room he entered with joy and energy.

 **Next on the roster was René Ezequiel "The Swag Kid" Rodriguez.** René was 13 when he joined the chess team in early 2015. He had an older brother and sister, but didn't know his father. There were occasions when he wouldn't be able to stay after school for chess practice because his mom was sick. In spite of his challenges, the kid had a lot of swag (oh, could that little guy dress up!). He had a different kind of swag than Pedrito (who was the cool cat). He played classical guitar and enjoyed composing. René's brother had played chess during the summer at Henderson, and René wanted to learn the game too.

RULE 4: Develop Your Pieces

 **Francisco Jesus "Frankie" Marquez** hadn't quite turned 12 years old when he joined the team as a sixth grader in early winter of 2014. He lived with his mother and a 19-year-old sister; his dad wasn't present in his life. Like most of the students, Frankie had family in Juárez. He was a gifted student. Unlike talkative Manny, Frankie was introspective, and even a bit eccentric. Watching him play chess was a trip! When he was in elementary school, he had gone to a chess program for a couple of weeks. Now he wanted to try again. All he had to overcome was his tendency to wander off.

 **Last, but NOT least,** of the final dynamic dozen was **Joshua Yosef Alvarado "Josh" Valero.** Josh was competent at chess, but he was also a star athlete and loved playing football, basketball, and soccer. His real interest level in chess was a little iffy. Time would tell.

My first job with the new Henderson Chess Club was to develop the team. I told them, "You guys do well enough and we will go to state. And if one or more of you win there, we'll travel to the nationals. If you do well there, I'll take you to a world tournament. We'll go to Germany or France or wherever it's being played. You'll travel the world."

They were thrilled with the idea of traveling outside of Texas and beyond America. Most had never even been out of El Paso.

The Champions' Game

"You'd really do all that for us, Mister?!"

"Yes. You guys do the work and I'll raise the money."

"And can we really get a college scholarship?"

Not very many people compete for chess scholarships, so it wasn't impossible to get one. A win at the nationals would most likely guarantee a student a scholarship into just about any college. But it wouldn't be easy. It all depended on how hard they worked. They would also have to become star academic students. They were already dealing with an awful lot in their lives, and had between zero and less than two years experience playing chess.

They were already pumped up, but I added a little bit more motivation. I told them about the Olympics. The Olympic Games were a couple of years away and this team wouldn't be able to qualify for 2016, but they could be ready by 2020, when they'd be in high school.

I told them, "They pick the top players from the United States to play against teams from other nations around the world. Any one of you could be on that team."

I explained that we wanted to do more than just travel and win awards. Our goal was to master the game of champions. Henderson was accomplishing things that others would never expect from kids from our side of I-10.

They looked at each other and grinned from ear-to-ear.

Time to get to work.

RULE 4: Develop Your Pieces

Putting together a championship team requires starting with the basics, even for those who have played before.

I start with the pawns, just moving them around the board, playing pawns against pawns.

In fact, my favorite life lesson is about pawns. You think of a pawn as just a lowly piece; after all it's only worth one point. But the reality is that in the endgame you'll often end up with only pawns and kings.

I told them, "If you don't know how to play the game with pawns, your game is going to be weak."

They learned several different pawn movements. One was the "pawn chain," in which a single pawn is the backbone and is protected by two other pawns, like kids sticking together for protection in rough areas of town. Another move is called a "pawn island," where the pawns help each other because they travel together. There is the "passed pawn," which is a pawn that travels from one side to the other and is transformed into the most powerful piece on the board, the queen. Finally, I described the "isolated pawn," which is a pawn that was all by itself. I compared this with street gangs.

"Every gang has a king. And that king tells everybody else—his pawns—exactly what to do. He can manage the pawns, he can tell them to go steal this, go take that, go tag up the walls. There are some pawns that will stick together—the traveling pawns—and will never get caught because they're always with each other. But there's always that one isolated pawn who no one cares about, whose dad is never there for him, whose mom is too busy for him, and who seems to be a loner. He's trying to get somewhere, but the king is controlling his every move. And yeah, that pawn can become a powerful queen if he makes it all the way across the board. But if not, what's going to happen? Since he's all by himself, he's going to get picked off. He's going to get captured—get thrown in jail."

The hands shot up in the air.

"So are we a pawn, Mister, or are we the king?"

"You should be a king, not somebody's pawn," I said. "You want to be the king controlling the board, calling the shots. And, you definitely don't want to be an isolated pawn."

Some people might think of Eduardo Retana as an isolated pawn. He was very quiet. In the classroom when he would do his work, he always preferred to be by himself. He would even ask if he could go outside because he said he focused better when he was alone.

Retana was very much into his Mexican culture, and because of that, he often felt out of step with the other kids. He preferred to speak mostly in Spanish. On top of that, he was a slow reader and received support from the special education program on campus.

While a lot of the kids spoke Spanish while practicing, I used English to share my stories and strategies. I taught them that by relating life experiences to chess, they would more easily grasp

RULE 4: Develop Your Pieces

the rules of the game. Once Retana became interested in the relationship between chess and life, his English began to improve.

Retana was very much into *narco corridos*, a style of music, which captures the reality of some segments of Mexican life (the same way hardcore gangster rap tells about another culture). However, these songs did not send positive and uplifting messages to a young man just entering the difficult teen years.

I could relate to Retana and his family. I was a Mexican-American myself and knew the feeling of coming into a school where there was a completely different culture. I knew how tough it was for him. He was rough around the edges. I understood that too, having been raised in Segundo Barrio. I could see the chess player developing in him, just as David Romo saw it develop in me.

After the team understood all about pawns, I threw in the king and had them play pawns against the king. Kings can only move one space at a time but can capture an opponent from any direction. Lose your king...game over!

Once the kids mastered that, I showed the power of rooks, that move in horizontal or vertical directions. I demonstrated how the bishops slide diagonally across the board. Fast and easy—the kids loved that.

Then I threw in the knights. The knights are the ones that jump forward two spaces and over one space. They're the only ones that can jump over other pieces. Because of this flexibility, the kids quickly adopted the knights as their favorite pieces on the board. "They are sneaky. You're playing along, and then... BAM, it gets you."

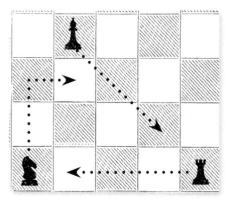

And last, I showed them the most powerful piece, the queen. The queen is agile. She can move anywhere she wants. As many squares as she wants. Go back and return. Diagonal, horizontal. She can make every move except the moves of the knight.

These were all pretty easy things to learn, because most kids enjoy games. What was more difficult, however, was teaching them how to *focus*. A big part of chess is learning how to concentrate, often for long periods of time during a game. To be able to sit quiet and still for an hour or two is almost impossible for middle schoolers. But there are ways that a child or an adult can learn to sit still for long periods of time—and not just sit still, but to *focus*.

I taught them to put a meaning or purpose to every move, rather than immediately acting. We started with five minute games and then we worked our way up...ten minutes...thirty minutes... until kids are able to play up to three hours. Slowly but surely, the kids learned to spend more time planning their moves.

RULE 4: Develop Your Pieces

The next lesson was to teach the students how to develop the individual chess pieces at the beginning of the game. This meant bringing the pieces into the game, moving them out of their starting positions, and into strategic positions. *All of them.*

I applied this to my coaching style as well—I don't have one best player, I have twelve. I develop all my pieces and build a deep bench.

Steven Mejía would eventually become a perfect example of how a deep bench could help win a tournament. Chess did not come easily to Steven. To be honest, he just wasn't that good. He had a difficult time winning and he would become disappointed when he lost. But his mom was always optimistic.

"Oh, I'm sure it just takes time," she would tell me whenever I updated her on his progress.

And it was taking time for Steven. In the beginning, I anticipated he would catch up fast, because his mother was a teacher and his parents were very supportive. But I was trying to shape a championship team with a deep bench. Students who weren't interested or who weren't getting it could be a drain on the rest of the team.

"Well, hopefully he'll catch up quickly," I would tell his mother.

He didn't.

But one thing I had learned was that everybody has their time. And one of Steven's best friends was Leo Gonzales. Being around a great player like that couldn't hurt.

"It'll be fine," his mother would tell me patiently. "We just want him to be involved in this great activity."

Everybody has their time.

Soon, I began to notice that the kids were always playing the fundamentals, sticking to the basics, the rules, and would get after each other for not doing things right.

"*¡Mira!*—you're not protecting your king."

Our deep bench would take us a long way. As one of them would drift, another would reel him in. *La unión hace la fuerza.*

I encouraged them to let go of their emotions and not worry about what was happening outside of the chess game. "Don't worry about what's happening with your family," I would tell them. "You guys can't fix everything that's going on at home. Things are what they are. Everything else has to fade back. The only thing that counts while you're playing is just you and the board.

> *¡Mira!* – **Look!**
>
> *La unión hace la fuerza* – **Strength in numbers**

PROTECT THE KING

In life we are taught that we must care for the "me" as well as the "we." In chess the king is the "me." All the other pieces are the "we." If you don't protect the "me," there is no "we" to worry about. The game is over.

Protect the king.

A good way to protect the king is to "castle" as soon as possible. Castling consists of switching the king with one of the rooks at the same time. This places the king in a protected position before it has even made its first move. This way, the king is protected from being checkmated or at least prevented from being put into a trap early in the game.

"It's like fortifying the castle—which is your house," I tell the kids.

The Champions' Game

Sometimes, during practice, they start saying, "Oh my God, I'm winning!"—and BOOM—a piece of theirs would suddenly get captured. Or they say, "Oh my God...I'm losing."—and BOOM—there goes another piece. It is a humbling experience, for sure.

I say, "Protect your emotions—your house—and be careful about who you let in. If you let somebody into your house—into your head—then they can get into your emotions, intimidate you, and affect your actions and reactions. So don't let them in. If you leave your castle open, you've lost the game. You have to protect the castle. You have to protect your emotions, your house."

"Do not allow yourselves to become nervous," I say. "You're there to play the game. Focus and move the pieces in a kind of zen-like way. Be fully present, but contain your emotions."

It isn't always emotions that get in the way. Sometimes kids face other challenges. For example, I noticed José Vanegas kept castling with his queen instead of his king. He had been playing chess long enough to know better, so I had to ask myself why he was making such a beginner's mistake. I talked to his mother and she revealed to me that he had a learning disability. It was then that I was able to understand why he was castling with the wrong piece. He was reversing the king and queen.

"What I want you want to do, *mijo*," I told José, "is to not touch the piece at all. Whenever you look at the board, train your brain to first make sure that's the piece you want to move. Think about it carefully and ensure your action matches your intention before you even touch the piece."

mijo – my son ✳

70

RULE 5: Protect Your King

Chess is not a race. Let the clock work for you, not against you.

José was very hard on himself. He wanted to be the best. When his learning disability cause him to would mess up a game, he would want to play again and again until he won. He ate, drank, and slept chess. He had to constantly wrestle through his disability.

Retana (the isolated pawn) also had a disability and was put in a resource classroom to get help with reading and math. It was really difficult for him to sit still in order to ponder his moves. I worked with him on this constantly, and enjoyed watching him make progress.

Frankie Marquez was dealing with loneliness and depression. Sometimes while waiting to get picked up after school, he would be sitting by himself, playing a game on his phone. We would invite him to come inside. While waiting with us, he admitted that sometimes he wasn't enjoying the game.

"I'm not having fun playing chess, Mister."

"Why not?"

"Because everybody's beating me."

"It takes time. You'll get it."

His concerns were so much bigger than chess. He worried because his mom struggled to earn enough money to take care of her two children. That was a lot of worry for a kid to be carrying on his shoulders. And unfortunately for him, things wouldn't get better anytime soon. It was dicey as to whether or not he would stick with chess at all.

The Champions' Game

Chris Carmona suffered from terrible migraine headaches. Yet he rarely told anyone when he was suffering one. His grandmother, who was raising him, had no means to pick him up when he got a migraine, so he would either walk home or find a quiet place to sleep it off. The headaches were scary for him. He knew when one was coming on because his vision in his left eye would blank out and he wouldn't be able to see. Then the pain would hit, and he couldn't be around light or noise for several hours unless he had his medication.

In spite of his medical challenge, Chris had an upbeat personality and was a successful student. He took to chess quickly, studied hard during chess club, finished all of his homework, went in on Saturdays, downloaded apps and practiced on his own. He approached his football and basketball playing with the same enthusiasm, intensity, and focus.

Some of the team members were in band or orchestra or had some other after-school activities. Their schedules were really full. Many took care of younger brothers or sisters and sometimes weren't able to show up to practice at all. Others had to leave early to pick up little brothers and sisters from elementary school, walk them home, and then walk back to practice. I really admired that in them. In spite of their individual challenges, they hung in there and helped each other out. At lunch break, they would have their chess books out and were busy helping each other work out problems. The kids were determined and resilient and amazing. The lessons on protecting the king resonated with the team.

As I began to see improvement in the team's play and my confidence in their ability increased, I decided it was time to road test them, to take them to little local tournaments to play against other kids at other middle schools.

I told them, "When we go to these local tournaments, there will be no more third place. It's time to win."

Sure enough, they shined. At the first local tournament of the new school year, they won first place. All the parents were snapping photos with their kids and their trophies. Tears were flowing everywhere—tears of joy.

"Why all the emotion?" I asked, confused. "It wasn't the state championship."

Okay, now was the time for emotions!

They said, "We know, Mister. But we've never won anything in our lives! And this is *first place*!"

What beautiful spirits. Cool on the boards like I had coached them to be, but celebrating the win like the middle schoolers they were! This was big. It was a mental game, and they had won.

Now it was also the time to push these kids to their limit, to see just how much they truly loved the game. To see what they could do.

I gave them the yellow tactics chess book that David Romo had given to me when I was a kid. Back when David gave it to me, we only had three months to complete all of the problems in it. I believed they could do it...faster.

The Champions' Game

"Here you go, guys," I told them. "There are close to one hundred pages in this book. You have three days to finish it. That's thirty pages a day. You can do this. Now get busy."

On the first day, I checked their progress. Every one of them had completed thirty pages.

Next day, "Here you go, Mister. Thirty more done."

And the crazy thing was, they kept showing up to practice. Every day. They *were* serious!

On the third day, thirty more done. I was blown away.

They wanted it badly. As a team, they had *ganas*.

As the spring competition loomed on the horizon, I prayed that my ragtag team of a dozen tough little Mexicans from south of I-10 could pull off a win at state. Because while their hearts and minds were top notch, they still had quite a few lessons to nail down.

ganas– the willingness to give your all

Sat-G/45 9:30 am	Sat-G/45 12:05 pm	2:25 pm	4:40 pm	
Sat-G/45 9:30 am	Sat-G/45 12:05 pm	Sat-G/45 2:25 pm	Sat-G/45 4:40 pm	Su 9
Sat-G/4 9:30 a	Sat-G/45	Sat-G/45 2:25 pm	Sat-G/45 4:40 pm	S

RULE 6

CHERISH YOUR QUEEN

Another rule in chess is similar to "protect the king." I call it "cherish your queen." If you want to lose fast, don't protect the king. But if you want to lose slowly and painfully, don't cherish your queen.

The queen can move anywhere she wants. As many squares as she wants. Go back. Return. Diagonal. Horizontal. She is tremendously agile and powerful. But, she has to be in her house, under protection. She's vulnerable if she's taken out too early in the game. Your opponent's pieces want to take out your queen and cripple your play. Once you are stripped of your queen, it's much easier to capture the king.

I taught the guys on the team to protect the only girl in the chess club, Lirio. After all, chess was a gentleman's game.

I had Lirio stand up and I told the boys, "This right here is our queen. You guys take care of her."

"And Lirio...right now, the boys in this chess club are your friends. Right now, these guys have absolutely nothing to offer you except their friendship. And guys, you have absolutely nothing to offer her. So let's focus on the game of chess. And if I hear there's any flirting going on, if I hear there's anything else but chivalry and chess going on, you'll be off the team."

At first, it was awkward for athletic guys like Manny to carry Lirio's backpack around at tournaments, or for a tough kid like Retana to walk her to her room when we traveled to tournaments, or for the guys to open the door for her at restaurants, and to keep her on the inside of the curb when we were walking (as protection from passing vehicles), and pull out her chair at restaurants. I didn't have them go as far as standing when she entered the room, but I was teaching them proper etiquette and good manners.

As long as there are boys on my chess teams, they will behave like gentlemen.

Lirio was a quiet, shy, very smart, and talented girl. She played in the school band. She would show up at chess club after school, play and practice, and then leave right away. She wanted to play chess and that's all. She never spoke to anyone, much less one of us adult males. When there were many other players in a room, she found it difficult to concentrate, so she would go to the bathroom or take a brief walk to settle herself.

As the year progressed, Lirio began to open up more as she went to more tournaments and met kids from other schools. She started having fun with her teammates. She liked their attentiveness and their sense of humor. She looked forward to chess club after school. Soon, the guys started seeing her as their little

RULE 6: Cherish Your Queen

sister to protect—no matter what. She was the queen of the team and they were cherishing their queen. They were becoming proper young gentlemen.

With the state tournament just a few months away, a teacher who had been volunteering to help with the team was suddenly transferred to another school. She had always been there, helping me with the team, doing anything we needed, and being the girls' chaperone. Now, I was all by myself.

I thought, "Who's going to help me drive? Who's going to help me with Lirio?"

Being a spiritual person, I talked to God and asked Him to send me the right person.

And did He ever.

Isela Anzaldo, the mother of two young children, was a special education teacher at Henderson and was also the school's volleyball coach. She enjoyed coaching fifteen-plus rowdy athletic girls on the volleyball team (who were all into boys), but wanted a counterbalance to all of those hormones. She had tons of positive energy and a fun sense of humor. She was patient. Given the chess team members emotional needs and special circumstances, Mrs. Anzaldo was a perfect fit for the job.

She told me that a roomful of quiet little chess intellectuals was just what she wanted.

Boy, was she in for a surprise!

RULE 7

EVERY MOVE HAS A PURPOSE

With all great chess players, success is directly related to purpose—there is a reason for every move. No randomness is involved. Every move contributes to the final checkmate, from the smallest move to the grandest play.

What happens if you lose a game? You are satisfied *if* you know that you've done everything possible, and acted with purpose. It's okay to lose games because you can learn from reviewing a game after it's done. If you do your best during the game, then you can ask no more of yourself.

Edna asked me once what my purpose was in putting so much time toward coaching the team.

RULE 7: Every Move Has a Purpose

"Are you doing this for chess?" she asked.

"No. It's not for chess," I told her. "Because if I just wanted to play chess and work on becoming a world champion, give me two years of intensive study and I'll become a world champion. My purpose is the kids. I do this to help build the next generation of people with purpose."

Everything I had done up to that point with the kids had one specific goal: to create champions.

As the state championship neared, I entered them in a tournament at Wiggs Middle School and told them, "Wiggs has had a team for two years. That means their players have more experience than you. But regardless of their experience, you guys can beat this team."

I figured we were in good shape. And sure enough, we beat Wiggs. Just by a little bit. Not much. Half a point. It was a squeaker. But that got me wondering, *Are we going to succeed at state or not?* I began to worry that they might not be ready to win at the state level.

After the Wiggs tournament, I told the kids, "We have a lot of work to do."

I had a lot of work to do, too, in addition to coaching. It was time to expand our support team beyond me and Mrs. Anzaldo.

I had to find a driver for the trip to McAllen, Texas, for the state championship. I also had to get the funds together to pay for the trip.

It wasn't easy to find the right people. People with the right energy, people who were positive, people who loved kids, people who were interested and dependable. People like Mrs. Anzaldo weren't exactly waiting in line to work extra unpaid hours after school and on weekends.

With twelve kids, me, another driver, and a chaperone for Lirio, we would need two vehicles. I could drive one, so I narrowed my focus to finding a driver for the second van.

I approached a teacher I thought might be interested and asked him, "Do you want to go to the state chess championships with us and help out?"

"Yeah, sure! Let's go!"

"Okay. It's going to be during the beginning of spring break."

"Oh...spring break? Really? Sorry, man. I can't."

"Why not?"

"It's my son. I have to spend time with him."

I asked another teacher and she said, "Let's do it!"

The next day she called me and said, "You know what? I can't do it. I'm sorry."

It was tough.

RULE 7: Every Move Has a Purpose

Then I approached Adrian Herrera, the school's burly Athletic Coordinator and AP teacher, who also happened to be a former professional player in arena football.

"Mr. Herrera, do you know how to drive a van?"

"Yeah, I do. What kind?"

"Twelve passenger."

"No problem."

"You want to go to the state chess championships in McAllen with me and the chess club?"

"Sure!"

I'd heard that before.

I was curious, so I asked him, "How do you like teaching Advanced Placement?"

"Oh—no, no. My AP stands for *Alternative* Placement. They're the kids who get in trouble."

"Oh. That AP. Okay, now I get it."

Mr. Herrera was big and gruff looking. He had a reputation as being the mean guy on campus. The disciplinarian. He could go to a classroom that was acting up or that had a substitute teacher and all he had to do was stare into the classroom, and all of a sudden you would hear, "Shhh! It's Mr. Herrera! Mr. Herrera!"

As I observed him, I noticed how easy it was for him to connect with the kids. That was his secret. If he could connect with children, he would be successful with them. He had been so successful, in fact, that he had actually fixed the school's alternative program. The kids there used to be rowdy, but as soon as he came onboard, he established discipline and connection. The kids knew he was there because he genuinely cared about them.

He and his wife, who was a counselor at a local school, had both earned master's degrees and were the parents of two boys, six and three years old.

He grew up in northeast El Paso in a hard-working, traditional Mexican-American family. He had two older brothers and a younger sister. His dad, a retired Army veteran who returned home from the Vietnam war disabled and with three Purple Hearts, was an electrical engineer. His mother was a stay-at-home mom. Finances were up and down and they struggled at times, but they made ends meet.

During the summers, Adrian worked at a ranch tossing bales of hay into a trailer. When he had time to go see a movie at the local theater, his mom would dig up some quarters from couches and chairs around the house and send him off.

He had been raised in a rough neighborhood where there were a lot of gangs. The town was divided along racial lines—blacks and Mexicans lived and associated separately. In school, Adrian was part of both cliques because he was an athlete and most of the black guys were athletes, and while some of the other Mexicans were troublemakers, they respected him for his size. I could

RULE 7: Every Move Has a Purpose

tell that the AP students both liked *and* respected Mr. Herrera, even though he was an authority figure.

He had everything I needed and wanted in an assistant and driver. Plus, it didn't hurt that he knew a little about chess. He agreed to join the team. And with just a few weeks until the state championships, he started right away, helping with my after-school chess training and working with the kids.

When I first told the chess team that the school's AP teacher, football coach, and athletic director was joining the team, they said, "Not him! He's *mean*, Mister! He's the AP teacher!"

They were used to seeing him as the disciplinarian. But after he went with us to one of the local tournaments, and goofed off with them, they began to see him in a whole new light. Now they were seeing him crack jokes, and trim the crust off of their bread as he made them sandwiches.

"Hey, he's not so mean, Mister!"

Over the next few weeks, Mr. Herrera got to know the kids. He was upbeat, yet could get them focused when they needed to settle down and practice. He was patient, fun, and dependable, had a relaxed, easy rapport with the students and quickly developed great relationships with them. When they needed a shoulder to cry on, they would go right to him. He turned out to be a big, cuddly, dependable teddy bear. With a goatee.

Whereas most of the kids saw me as a father figure, they saw Mr. Herrera as more of a big brother or uncle. As a father himself, his approach with the team was the same as mine. He lifted them up. He encouraged them. He cared about them. He would do anything necessary for their well-being.

By early 2015, the kids were busy learning the more advanced lessons, one of which is the importance of planning their next move in advance—even before they are about to make their current move. One method to do that is what's called "discover attacks," a tactic that involves moving pieces in a way that forces an opponent to make a specific move.

For example, if your opponent's moves are setting you up for an attack, you move one of your pieces in such a way that the opponent knows that if he attacks you, it will cost him. It's about thinking ahead, anticipating, planning, and moving with purpose.

There are basically two types of players: the player who just moves pieces with no plan or purpose, and the player who plays tactics. Tactics differ from strategy in that a strategy is an overall plan for the game, whereas tactics are the little moves within that overall strategy that make it work. As soon as you learn the tactics, your game changes completely. Without purpose and planning, you're going somewhere, but you don't know where. Having no purpose and plan is like living a life that meanders from one thing to the next without meaning.

Part of the plan has to include dealing with your weaknesses. For example, Frankie had a tendency to get so nervous in the beginning of a tournament that it would affect his play until he settled into his strategy. He would win one round, and lose the next. He was inconsistent. When he was on, he was good. But when he was off, he was awful. He also tended to get overcon-

RULE 7: Every Move Has a Purpose

fident in the third round, but in the fourth he would get very serious. I had him work on pacing himself, calming himself, deliberately slowing down and taking his time.

Despite any weaknesses within the team, all the kids were dedicated. For example, Manny and Chris would sometimes do their problem-solving homework together at Manny's house until two in the morning. Chris would get home at three in the morning, sneak in quietly and go to bed, only to have to get up for school at six the next morning.

These kids wanted one thing only: to win.

I pushed them hard to do even better. I was strict, but it was for their own good.

We practiced every day but Sunday and went to as many local competitions as possible. Soon, these kids were playing against each other at these tournaments because they had become so good they were beating everyone else.

The team was on its way to becoming a well-oiled chess machine. They were just about ready to take on the state of Texas.

KNOW WHEN TO W

DON'T JUDGE BY

SACR

EXPE

NEVER GIVE UP

RULE 8

KNOW WHEN TO WALK AWAY

Sometimes, in a game, you need to step away from your plan and redirect. It's a difficult concept to grasp, but sometimes the best strategy is actually to walk away. Picture this: You are directing your strategy to where you think your opponent's king is going to be...but then he decides to castle. Suddenly, you need to rearrange your pieces. The panic sets in. You can't let it get to you. You need to bring your pieces back, retreat, and prepare to attack again.

When you can't see a solution, step away. Walk away from the board. Get a "fresh pair of eyes" to look at the situation. Get up. Move. Stand next to your opponent and look at the board from his or her point of view and a solution may stand out. It may make your opponent nervous; you may even feel awkward standing there. But you will be able to see things from a new perspective. You may have been preparing to exchange pieces, but now you realize that retreat is a better strategy...for now.

But it's not always easy to walk away from some things.

RULE 8: Know When to Walk Away

When I entered middle school, I had to make certain decisions. Living in a tough neighborhood like Segundo Barrio, the time would come when I'd have to decide whether or not to join a gang. I could continue going to school, but when I went to school I could get bullied. It was not cool to be smart. If I even carried books, I risked getting beaten up by gang members. So carrying books wasn't an option for me. I learned to memorize everything that was written on the board.

Even though I wasn't carrying my books, I had something else stacked against me. I played chess. And chess was *not* cool.

So I had a decision to make. I had to decide whether I wanted to join a gang. Joining a gang would mean selling drugs and doing a lot of illegal activities. But it also would mean respect—being cool. At that point, one of my family members, "El Johnny", helped to open my eyes. He admitted he was currently very involved in gangs.

He told me, "This is not a lifestyle for you." And when I heard that from a well-respected gang member, it made me think twice as to what steps to take next.

He said, "You're *going* to continue school, you're *going* to finish, and you're *going* to be very successful."

Joining a gang, though, was more or less expected. It meant *respect*, and that was what I wanted. But earning that respect came with a price. Whether it was through selling drugs, beating people up or...doing whatever you have to do. You *earned* respect. El Johnny was highly respected, and I wanted to be just like him. He was my role model.

But, when my "role model" told me that he was NOT a role model, it opened my eyes.

That's when I decided to walk away. Retreat, and try a new strategy.

The decision to walk away lead me to meeting my new friends, my chess family. That's when I became good friends with Nacho, among others. As friends, we all continued to spend time together, and then in high school, we won the State Championship.

None of this would have happened if I didn't make the choice to walk away.

I chose school. I chose chess.

As I was getting the team ready for the 2015 state competition, I noticed they were becoming increasingly nervous and hesitant about the impending trip to McAllen. Their nervousness was understandable. It was going to be a brand new experience for them. They had never traveled before. They had never competed at such a high level. I knew how they felt, because I had been in the same situation when I was in middle school and had begun to expand out into the world through chess competitions.

I told Mrs. Maldonado we needed to do something to help the team calm down.

"I think I have the right person for you," she said.

RULE 8: Know When to Walk Away

I didn't know there was such a thing as people who calmed kids down for a living, but she was convinced this person could help.

"There's a lady my sister knows who wrote a book about seeing dead people. She can teach the kids some relaxation and motivation techniques."

Oh...oh kaaay, I thought. *Where is this going?*

"Seeing dead people?" I said. "That sounds, uh...very interesting."

"You're gonna like her. Her name is Mrs. Cromer."

So we set it up for the dead people-seeing Mrs. Cromer to come in and motivate the kids. At least it sounded...very entertaining.

Mrs. Cromer brought the kids snacks from McDonald's.

"I can't do this if the kids are not well fed," she explained as the students ate their snacks.

When they were finished eating, she gathered the kids around her and told them, "I'm going to teach you to leave everything behind. Everybody close your eyes."

The kids shut their eyes.

"You are walking across this huge room. Imagine it in your mind. You go to the door and open it. You step outside, close the door, and keep on walking. There's a beach, with a river running by it. Just picture it. And right there, on the beach, at the river, you leave all your problems. Everything that causes you pain. Everything. If you're scared, you leave it right there in that big place. Pile everything right there on the beach. Now you see a big balloon floating there. Tie everything to the balloon...and let it go. Just release it into the sky and watch it float far away over the water."

Apparently the kids had done that, because by that point, they were all smiling...eyes shut tight, imagining their problems drifting away.

"Okay, now walk away from the beach, go back to the door, open it and step back into the classroom. Now, close the door... and you're here. Open your eyes."

When the kids opened their eyes, they looked peaceful and calm. She did a couple of other exercises with them and the kids became completely different. There was an air of peaceful self-confidence about them. Apparently, they had left their troubles down by the river.

Then she said, "Now, when you guys go to play an opponent in chess, you make them your..." She paused a moment, looking as if she was deciding whether or not to say the next part.

All of a sudden, I caught onto where she was going with it and I started thinking to myself, *Don't say it, don't say it!—this is a school, these are kids! Don't say it!*

"You make them your—" and she finished the sentence, using the one word that should never complete that sentence.

¡Ay Diosito!—she said it! I thought, looking at Mr. Herrera.

> *¡Ay Diosito!–*
> **Oh dear God!** ✱

RULE 8: Know When to Walk Away

The kids started laughing hysterically.

Both Mr. Herrera's and Mrs. Maldonado's jaws dropped.

The students loved the whole motivation seminar. And now they had an image in their minds that could get them through anything. With a knowing grin on their faces.

These kids were ready to make Texas their...you know what.

RULE 9

DON'T JUDGE by APPEARANCE

B y March of 2015, the twelve members of the team were ready for McAllen and the state tournament. There was only one catch: we only had enough funding to take nine players. I needed to decide who would stay at home, and who would go.

First, I looked at the team members who simply could not go. Right off the top, Frankie wasn't going. His level of play just wasn't good enough at the time. He was a gifted kid, but he wasn't a solid team player. Not yet, anyway.

Next, I had to look at the kids who didn't seem to really want to go. Josh was at the top of that list because he had been so involved in different sports that he was neither ready nor fully available to go.

RULE 9: Don't Judge by Appearance

The final cut made itself. It would either be René or Manny. Manny's play had been a little iffy lately, and René was a better player in some circumstances. But René ended up disqualifying himself from going because he failed a class. I would have to tell René that he couldn't go, and that he'd better get his grades up or he wouldn't be going to the nationals either, if the team did well at state.

However, I wouldn't tell René that just yet. Not until I told Manny that the slot was his. But I decided that before I would tell him, I'd make sure he really wanted it. He would have to work for it.

"Manny, I might have a spot open for the trip to state, but it's between you and someone else. If you win this next local tournament, you get to go to state."

"Really, Mister?!"

I had his attention.

Sure enough, at the tournament, Manny started winning all of the rounds. He was down to the last round. Then he got nervous, realizing he was on the verge of clinching a spot at state.

He went to the restroom. He was pacing back and forth, rubbing his knuckles, wiping his palms on his pants.

He was taking so long, I went in.

"You okay, buddy?"

"Oh my god, Mister, oh my god, I'm gonna win. I'm gonna go to state."

"It's not over yet, *mijo*. Calm down. You're too nervous. Control your center, boy."

He suddenly rushed into a stall and slammed the door.

"You alright in there?"

"I'm good, Mister."

Then all of a sudden I heard a loud, *"RAAAAAAGH!"* as he started throwing up.

Sure enough, he lost the round.

But there was something about Manny Tejada. He just made everybody happy.

I put him on the team for state.

This meant that officially on the roster to go to state were: Pedro Escobar, Eduardo Retana, Leo Gonzalez, Steven Mejia, Lirio Gomez, José Vanegas, Brandon Caballero, Christopher Carmona, and Manny Tejada. I promised all twelve chess club members that if we did well at state and qualified for the nationals, the entire group would go.

But it was a promise that would be almost impossible to keep.

Whenever we traveled to play in championships, I always made sure we stayed at nice hotels, because the better ones usually had the best swimming pools and the kids loved swimming. I also tried to arrive a day before the competition started so we could go sightseeing. The majority of the kids on my chess teams had never traveled outside of El Paso. Arriving early and staying at a nice hotel allowed them time to relax in the pool and take a leisurely tour of the town. That way, they would feel more alert and focused, and ready to play.

We drove in two vans to McAllen. It was quite a road trip; fourteen hours in all. We passed the time by playing elimination chess on our little magnetic chessboard and we always had music playing.

The low music and the sound of the tires on one particular endless stretch of flat, boring Texas plains had lulled the kids to sleep when suddenly, Manny yelled from the back of the van, "Hey, Mister, we gotta play something fast to get us going!"

Manny was a character. He was the spirit of the Henderson Chess Club.

So we turned on Mrs. Anzaldo's Zumba® class music and the kids woke up and Manny really started going to town, dancing in the back. Everyone was clapping as he did little twists and turns. Suddenly it was a party bus, rolling across Texas.

Eventually, they wore themselves out and everyone but Lirio drifted back to sleep.

She smiled as she watched the boys splayed across each other, snoring and drooling as we rumbled south, deeper into Texas, headed toward the Gulf of Mexico.

Lirio and her older sister lived with their mom—who was an amazing person. Her mom and sister drove behind our bus all the way to McAllen to watch Lirio compete. No other parent did that with their kid on the team. She was always there for Lirio.

And that would soon cause real complications.

By the end of our long travel day, I was exhausted. It was mentally and physically challenging to travel with so many children to competitions, then make sure everything was okay at the hotel, get everybody unpacked, and fed and in bed. And then out of bed early the next morning, and fed, and dressed, and to the competition. And supported, and coached, and pumped up during play. And then take them all to dinner afterward. It was a draining experience that wore me out.

By the time we arrived at the hotel, I had been up from seven in the morning until ten that evening. I was sore. My body ached. My brain hurt. I was physically drained, mentally drained, emotionally drained. Just dealing with the highs and lows of children's emotions alone was exhausting enough. By the time we got to the rooms, I was a zombie. I was so tired that I lay on the floor and dozed off.

Far off in the sleepy haze of my mind, I could hear Mrs. Anzaldo pumping the kids up to play a game of chess with her.

"Come on, guys. Let's play a game."

"But you don't even know how to play chess, Miss."

"Oh, no, you're wrong about that. I can play chess."

RULE 9: Don't Judge by Appearance

Then she proceeded to actually beat a couple of them and I thought, *Wow, she's taking over. This is nice. I can actually take a nap.* But then my mind started going to work on me. Mrs. Anzaldo knew the mechanics of the moves and she was smart. But she was not a chess player, not really. More of a patzer. But if she was able to beat some of these kids, who had been trained by me and were on their way to compete at the state level...

¡Ay Diosito!, are we in trouble? Can the kidzzzzzz ...Thank God, before I could finish the thought, I fell asleep, feeling thankful that she, Mr. Herrera, and I had gotten the team all the way to McAllen.

The Texas Scholastic Chess Championships were held in McAllen, Texas, on March 28, 2015.

At the convention center where the tournament was held, the teams had the option to rent hospitality rooms for the coaches to wait in during the rounds. The players could practice and relax, make phone calls, eat snacks, and drink beverages in these rooms, but they were expensive. It was a financial struggle to travel with a large group like ours. We wanted to have nice rooms to sleep in, but we couldn't afford any of the extras.

We'd barely had enough money to get to the tournament in the first place, so we stayed out in the hallway and practiced on the floor. It was uncomfortable hanging out there in the hallway. But we weren't there for the luxury. We were there to win.

The Champions' Game

Inside the playing hall at the convention center, my team's nervousness was written all over their faces. They felt they were the youngest, the shortest, the skinniest, the smallest. To them the other players were big, older, and scary. It was like they had entered a biblical land of giants. When you're in sixth grade, a seventh grader can seem huge, and an eighth grader massive.

On day one, the tournament venue was packed. The kids saw players of other nationalities and ethnicities strolling around that they had never seen before. For them, it was like a scene out of *Star Wars* with all sorts of odd beings strolling past them in human clothes. They saw stern, inscrutable Asian kids who didn't say a word and never made a face. They saw kids wearing fancy blazers with kangaroo logos on the breast, with a little motto beneath it that said *"Checkmate. Good game!"* They saw tall black kids who towered over everyone else, taller than any other middle-schooler they'd seen before.

"Wowww...they're *big*, Mister!"

"We're playing against *these guys*, Mister?"

"They're mean looking, Mister."

"Don't judge a book by its cover," I said.

I had taught them to never judge by appearance—one of my biggest rules, especially with the racism that exists in America. I taught them that it didn't matter how old they were, how young they were, how tall, short, skinny, heavy, wide, what color, what gender. Because you never know who you're going to beat. Or who's going to beat you.

I stood at the front of the door to the tournament area where the kids would come out after they had played. After each round, they would give me their game-play sheet and I would go over their games to see how they did and to help them analyze how they could beat their opponents.

Retana was scared when he realized who his first opponent was. When we walked into the room and saw the boy he was going to be playing, he yelled, "No way! There's no way I can beat this guy." He was African-American, over six feet tall, and towered over Retana. But in the end, Retana won.

After that match, a little bit of gloating set in. He started mocking his extra tall opponent in front of me.

I had to warn him.

"You know, Retana, you shouldn't be saying things like that. Karma could come and get you!"

"No way, Mister, it never will!" Retana was quite sure of himself.

But sure enough, it did get him.

Later, Retana was given a second chance to learn not to judge by appearances. This time, his opponent looked like a second grader. A much smaller Asian student, who also happened to have a broken leg. She even had to use a walker. None of us had ever seen a little girl with a walker before. The kids started pointing and laughing.

The Champions' Game

"Hey Mister, look at that girl with the walker!"

I thought to myself, it was not right to make fun of this poor girl like this. So I said to my students, "Guys, I wouldn't do that if I were you. Remember, you don't play with your leg, you play with your head." I even told them, "Man, she looks happy, she probably won her last match."

A few hours later, Retana came out from a game and found us. He looked terrible.

I asked him, "What's wrong, Retana?"

"I lost, Mister."

"Who'd you lose to?"

He put his head down, "The little girl with the walker."

The kids hollered, "Oh, no way! Retana!" Everybody started laughing, he started tearing up, and they were like, "Oh, man!"

I told him, "Remember when you played that big guy?"

"Yeah, Mister."

"Never judge by appearance, Retana. Never."

In chess, the players try to get inside each other's heads. For example, while thinking about their own move or waiting for their opponent to move, some of the kids could sit as still as a

RULE 9: Don't Judge by Appearance

marble statue for two hours. I was proud of my kids for being able to focus for a full hour without fidgeting. But some of their opponents would stare at them like they were looking through them, and that could get on the kids' nerves.

Or an opponent might say something casual to them like, "How long have you been playing?"

"Oh, just one year," the Henderson kid would reply.

"I've been playing since I was two," the opponent would say.

"Wow—*really?*"

"Yeah. Good luck."

I trained the kids to ignore these tactics.

"They're just trying to annoy you and throw you off your game," I told them. "Chess is a mind game. Don't let them get inside your head."

Just smile. Nod. Be pleasant. Maybe respond with something brief, like, *Wow. Really? Playing since you were in diapers, huh? Did it get messy?*

But the best way to get inside an opponent's head was to simply outplay them.

When Retana had seen his first opponent, the guy was already in Retana's head just by his appearance alone. Retana had become instantly intimidated and they hadn't even shaken hands yet.

Don't judge by appearance.

Chris had a similar experience. To Chris, who was only 13, his opponent looked like he was at least 16. He was big, he was older.

When Chris saw the guy as he was about to go in, his face flushed red and he said, "Oh my God, he's so big, Mister. I'm about to lose!"

"Chris, remember: it's not how he looks. It's how he plays. Just do your best."

The game took two hours and five minutes and ended in a tie. Chris felt like he'd gone twelve rounds with a giant. And *didn't* lose.

When I used to play in high school and college, I was afraid of the Asian players. I remember one time when I had played an Asian kid at the nationals in Louisville, Kentucky. I thought, *Ah, man... he's gonna beat me.* That was just my perception. *Asians are better than me. Caucasians are better than me.* All that stuff has no basis in reality, and is just put into our heads by artificial means and through our experiences of racism.

Then I started playing him. And I realized I was better than him. And I realized that all that programming in my head was completely wrong.

Perhaps my biggest lesson in life about judging by appearance occurred the summer after my second year as a teacher. I had presented at a multimedia art workshop at The University of Texas at Austin (UT Austin) with a teacher friend of mine. When we walked into the room, seated around a long table were twenty people. Out of all of those, my friend and I were the only Mexican-Americans. Everybody else was white.

The instant we stepped into that room, everybody looked us over from head to toe.

My friend leaned into me and whispered, "Man, why'd you bring me here?"

"Just hold on. Let's see what this is about."

We sat down and everybody started talking about their school and their district. We were thinking, *These guys are superior to us.* It was just a natural reaction—*What're we doing here?*

But we stayed.

Each teacher did their presentation. I was last.

My multimedia presentation was a short video I had produced that was less than two minutes long, titled, "The Final Move." It was about chess and my life. I had put it together on iMovie. The workshop had been about putting a life story together with multimedia such as video, audio, and photographs. It had taken me less than half an hour to produce and it contained a simple message: chess had given me opportunities and opened doors to me as a student that I never would have experienced otherwise. The video described what chess taught me:

To any problem, there is a solution, no matter how hard it might seem.

Sometimes I have to sacrifice to win.

I have options in life. I can travel extensively and get an education through chess.

My dreams can come true—including graduating from college and working in a career that I chose for myself; helping children create paths for their own dreams.

That was it. Eighty-eight seconds. The group loved it. I was asked by the facilitator to teach the others at the workshop about how to put together multimedia art presentations. In the end, the dean of the fine arts program at UT Austin told me that they would take anyone into the art program whom I recommended, because I had proven myself.

At that moment I realized the power of the mind. It was all in my head. What I thought about people who could do better than me was simply an implanted mindset. It could just as easily be exchanged for a more positive and healthy one. It was a matter of choice.

When I had gone to chess tournaments before that workshop, my mindset was:

"Oh, we're playing Asians."

"Ah, we're playing Indians."

"Chihuahua, we're playing whites. We're not gonna beat them."

"Dios mío, we're playing New York! God, those guys are just way better than us!"

"Oh no—we're playing Brownsville! They've had a team for 15 years. They'll destroy us!"

RULE 9: Don't Judge by Appearance

No more!

After my UT Austin experience, I had come back and told my kids at Henderson, "We are going to McAllen. And we are going to win."

They said, "But we've never been to a state championship before, Mister."

"That's alright. We're gonna beat them. You have a brain, too. You've trained yourself. You've practiced very hard. And I'm sure they have, too. But we'll see who has practiced more."

That workshop had changed me completely. I now knew...and I believed...race and economic status have nothing to do with what a person is capable of accomplishing.

As round one progressed, the team was struggling. It was hard at state tournaments, because even though the kids were inside the room, and you still see them, you could not observe their moves. I knew they were struggling, though, because I could read their body language and the expressions on their faces.

Heading into state, Lirio had been one of our stronger players. I was convinced that she was going to be in the top four overall. I had even told Mr. Herrera, "Lirio is going to be battling with Leo and Chris for the top spot."

I was expecting her to give everyone a good run for their money. But I was surprised when I could tell by watching Lirio's face that she had lost all focus. She was so nervous, she was someone else. She was breaking all the rules. Forgetting all the principles of an opening. Playing below beginner's level.

I wondered if part of her nervousness and lack of focus might have something to do with her mom being there. As nice and attentive as her mother was, it seemed that her being at the tournament might be a distraction for Lirio. This was a competition and kids behaved differently during stressful times like this when they needed to focus. It was like any public game. When you have too many people watching, it makes a child very nervous. But having your mom there could make it even worse.

When the round ended, Lirio burst out of the door so distraught that she ran, crying, straight to the girls' bathroom devastated by her first-round performance.

Her mother ran in after her.

After about half an hour, Lirio kicked her mom out of the bathroom.

Her sister went in. After twenty or thirty minutes, she too was tossed out.

Then Mr. Herrera, big brother to the kids, the teddy bear, the fun guy who could get them to relax no matter what, went to the door and tried to talk her out.

She wouldn't budge.

Her mother said to me, "Mr. Ramirez, it looks like she wants to go home. We're going to leave now."

RULE 9: Don't Judge by Appearance

"Wait," I said, "This is only the first round. She has plenty of time to improve. Let me talk to her."

"Well...she's in the girls' restroom and she's not coming out."

I called Mrs. Anzaldo over and said, "Will you please go in there and talk to her?"

Mrs. Anzaldo went in. She didn't come out for nearly an hour. By then, Lirio had been in the girls' restroom for two hours.

I stood close to the door and said, "Lirio, this isn't about how you played—you'll get plenty of chances to do better, and you will do better. We know that. But you can't quit, because this is about the team. You lost individually in the first round, but we're here for the team and there are more rounds ahead."

Finally, after three hours that felt like two days, she came out.

Like I said, somebody always cries at the tournaments. Just usually not that long.

I asked her, "Lirio, did you have fun today before the first round?"

"Yeah, it was fun, Mister."

"Good. I had fun, too. We all had fun. You're very fun to be with. The reason I want you to play chess is for you to have fun and enjoy yourself and make friends. I didn't bring you here just to play chess to win the state tournament. I didn't bring you just so you would be the winner. If you do win, then, wow—that's amazing. But if you don't, you're having a good experience, right?

The Champions' Game

You're meeting new people, making new friends, and traveling. Right?"

"Yes. I love it."

"Well, that's exactly what you're gonna do from now on, *mija*. You're gonna go in there and you're just gonna have fun and nothing else. If you lose, who cares? As long as you have fun. I don't care if you win or lose. I only want you to have fun. *¿Bien?*"

"Yes, Mister."

It was a roundabout way to tell her to never quit, but in her fragile emotional condition it was important that she understood that there was no requirement to win. She did not have to perform for the happiness of the adults; just play with the happiness of a kid.

I had taught the kids that in chess they should never give up. Even if they were down to just the king standing alone on the board, don't quit.

I learned this when I had won the State Championship in 2001. I had been losing the last round, and had only my king and one rook left on the board.

I reached my hand out to my opponent and said, "I offer you a draw."

A draw meant that we could each walk away with half a point.

¿Bien?– okay?

✳

108

RULE 9: Don't Judge by Appearance

He said, "Do you see the board? I'm winning."

"I understand that. Do you want to draw?"

"No."

Right then I remembered what David Romo had taught me: *never give up, never stop fighting, never quit.*

Thinking, *Let's see what destiny brings,* I said, "Fine."

Sure enough, the next move, he made a blunder and gave me a rook.

He looked up suddenly, held out his hand and said, "I'll take your draw."

"No. Not anymore."

The next move, we traded rooks. Then I ended up taking a pawn. And he lost the game.

What that experience had taught me, as a young man in high school on the cusp of launching out into life, was to never give up, even when it's just your king all by himself. Because your opponent may make a mistake. Everybody makes mistakes. You may be competing against someone in sports and you think they have the lead. But you never know, he might trip. In a company, you never know. You might think you have made a big sale, then something happens and the buyers pull out. You never know. So, never quit.

You never know.

The Champions' Game

When Lirio was calm enough, and decided to keep playing, I had to get her head back in the game. So I analyzed her board with her and went over her moves.

I said, "What were you thinking with this move, Lirio?"

"I wasn't thinking, Mister."

"Yeah, I can see that."

I pointed out each of her first three moves.

"Why'd you play this move?"

"I don't know, Mister. I was nervous."

"Why'd you play this move?"

"I don't know, Mister."

"Remember, Lirio, every move must have a purpose."

"I know, Mister. I remember."

"Look, there's no point for you to keep going if it's not you playing the game. You're one of my very best players. So you have to refocus yourself."

I explained to her that she needed to attack more.

"Don't hold back so much, Lirio. Act instead of react."

"I can do it, Mister."

It was hard for Lirio when she lost at chess, especially if the players were ranked the same or lower than her. Her problem was that she usually liked to play defense more than offense because she tended to be passive, so it could be challenging to make the bold moves necessary to rout an opponent.

Instilling fear in the person across from you in a competition wasn't just about being from a school whose chess team had won a previous state tournament, it was about delivering the goods on the board. Lirio hadn't been a champion yet. She didn't have the badge to flash and the fear to instill in her opponents. Not yet. That, she would have to earn.

To become a champion takes time and effort. But she would get there. Loud and clear.

After that first round, Lirio had been ready to go home. And her mom was ready to take her. But Mrs. Anzaldo had talked to her. Then I had talked to her. And we had managed to convince Lirio that she was going to be alright.

Lucky for us (and especially for Lirio), the experience taught her mother a lesson. She had been expecting this trip to be a time for her and her daughters to travel together and do fun things with Lirio during the tournament. But that was not what Lirio was there for. Lirio was there to play in an important competition. Not to have fun with Mom. Not to play with her sister.

Lirio's mother realized that the best thing she could do would be to back off and give Lirio space to do what she had come to do. After she figured that out, her attitude changed like day and night, and she was able to be there for Lirio in a far more emotionally empowering way. She let Lirio be the competitive player that she needed to be.

Lirio had gotten her game together after her first-round disaster, but some of the boys were playing a little too fast and it was costing them.

I got everyone together for a pep talk and said to them, "You guys need to slow down and take your time. Everybody relax and visualize. Dump all your stress on the beach, tie it to the balloon, and let it all go. Visualize your win. You remember what Mrs. Cromer taught you, right?"

"Yes, Mister."

"You go in there, you shake your opponent's hand, and you tell them with your eyes, *I'm here to beat you.*"

"Yeah, Mister!"

"Now go back in there and take your time. I need you guys to be playing for at least an hour in there."

"Okay, Mister!"

Then I walked them back to the tournament area, and Mr. Herrera and Mrs. Anzaldo and I wished them good luck, told them to concentrate, and reminded them to take their time.

"We'll see you when you're done with the next round."

RULE 9: Don't Judge by Appearance

The reason I wanted them to stay at each game for at least an hour was because when they played fast, they were more vulnerable to making a mistake. But it frustrated them sometimes when their opponent would take half an hour to make a move while staring at the board, or up at the ceiling as if rigor mortis had set in. These were just 12- and 13-year-old little kids. I had trained them to sit still for an hour, but they were still children and had only so much attention span to go around before they would become impatient and frustrated. A minute can feel like an hour. An hour can feel like five minutes. Eventually, the kids grow tired and impatient. They want to go home, and get in their own bed, and watch their own TV, and play their own video games. It is at *this* point that they become most prone to making a mistake like playing too fast.

That's why, in the last round of the tournament, it becomes even more crucial to control the game by taking your time. If you have two minutes left to make a move, you can control right up to the last five seconds before you move. It is all psychological. A mind game. It is crucial that they learn to master the ability to be patient. Besides, what good things in life don't require patience?

I told them, "Remain still. Time will go slow. Sit there calmly and don't worry, but don't lose sight of the time."

As I was walking back to our place in the hallway after my little pep talk, Steven caught up to me and was walking right behind me.

The Champions' Game

I turned and said, "Do you need something, Steven?"

"No, Mister. I lost."

"You *what??*—you weren't even in there five minutes!"

"I think I played my best, Mister."

"You think you played your best? Dude, I just sent you in and now you're coming out. And that's your best? Didn't I just tell you, *take your time?*"

I was really upset with him. So he took out his board and started playing the game, reviewing his moves.

"Why are you trying to review your play?" I barked at him. "You just played a five-minute game, Steven. There's nothing to review! You just gave up!"

I was being so strict on him that I called his mom and told her, "You know what, ma'am, this kid is just messing around. He's not interested in the tournament."

"Well, you can yell at him and you can tell him whatever you want, Mr. Ramirez. Just get him straight."

"Okay. You said it."

So I did. I gave him a real Mexican ear-beating.

And it worked. He was afraid to lose from then on.

¿Qué pasa?–
what's happening?

RULE 9: Don't Judge by Appearance

An hour after Steven's loss, Chris came out. Beaming with excitement he treaded over to us. I asked him, "*¿Qué pasa,* Chris? How did you do?"

He yelled, "Mister, I did it—I won!"

"How do you feel?"

"Mister, I made him my *female dog!*"

The other coaches around us all turned and looked at us like we were thugs from the barrio that had snuck in a side door.

I grinned sheepishly at the coaches (*kids—what're you gonna do?*), grabbed Chris and hugged him close to me and told him under my breath, "Man, don't say that. The coaches are gonna think we're teaching you guys this."

"But I beat him, Mister! I beat him!"

"I know that, it's awesome. But this is a gentleman's game."

Finally, they were adapting and settling in.

By the end of the first day of competition, the kids' play had improved and they were doing pretty well. Almost all of them had two or three wins and only one loss.

We had a long way to go. But we had a chance.

RULE 10

SACRIFICE

In chess, it's important to be able to assess whether to sacrifice a piece in order to accomplish a bigger goal. I taught the team to exchange a high-value piece for a lower one so they could get an even higher one in a couple more moves. Some strategies require you to give up a piece if sacrificing will give you the best result in the game. If it was going to lead to checkmate, then you make the sacrifice.

For example, when I was a teenager, checkmate in my life plan was to finish my college education. If that plan required that I sacrifice by living in subsidized housing and take government assistance, then so be it. Whatever it took to win. If raising a young child with my wife while we were going to school full time was required to achieve my goal, then the sacrifice was worth it.

When we attended UTEP, it would be four years of sacrifice if we followed our plan to earn our degrees. Otherwise, it would be a lifetime of regret if we didn't sacrifice to finish college. For me and Edna, it was a no-brainer: go to school, make the necessary but temporary sacrifices, and finish the plan. Whatever it takes to win.

But it wasn't easy. It was much harder for Edna to stick with the plan, because (being a mother and a wife) she wanted to have a comfortable home for our young son, and that took more money. And money took work. And work took away from school. So, there was a powerful temptation for her to switch her coursework to a six-month medical assistant certificate and then go get a job. I understood that.

Edna said to me, "Let me do something that I'm going to complete in a few months. Then I can start working. I can always go back and finish college later."

I told her, "But we already decided to complete school first."

It was difficult because we were living with Edna's mom.

I would hear her mother tell her, "Just do the six-month thing, Edna. Get it done. Then go get a job."

Basically, that meant quit school and go get a job at not much above minimum wage with little future of upward career prospects in order to ease our temporary discomfort. In chess, that would be like taking a pawn just because it's right there in front of you, without looking to see how the move might affect your game a move or two later. It's not always best to take the short-term, easy way out just to avoid making a sacrifice that will pay off in bigger, future gains.

Still, it was hard for Edna to have me on one side saying, "We need to stick to our plan and stay in school." Her mother on the other side was saying, "Why would Saul want you to go through this hardship for so many years? Go to school just for a few months and get a certificate. It's going to be good for you and your son."

It was a battle of mindsets on which way to best approach setting up our entire lives together. Just as in chess, where a game can last several hours or even days, I learned that life is about adapting to the long game—a game with only one goal in mind: checkmate. Not a draw. Not a loss. A complete win.

It was difficult for Edna, feeling she was being forced to make a decision between me and her mom, who was giving her opposite advice. But Edna and I were building our lives together; it was time to cut the cord and do what would ultimately be best for the family. It was just as hard for me, because as a man, and a husband, and a father, it was tempting to quit school, go get a job and start bringing in some money to support my family right away.

But we had laid out our plan and I was going to play it through. Yet, I knew that as soon as she got the prerequisite courses out of the way and entered nursing school, it was going to become

RULE 10: Sacrifice

even harder for her. The sacrifices would be hard, but we would be there for each other all the way. It's all a matter of determining in advance if the sacrifice will be worth the results.

Sometimes, sacrifice means not getting what we want for the sake of those we love and care about. For example, before I had left for the 2015 Texas State Chess Championship, my son, Saulito, began expressing a sudden interest in chess. But for him to move to my school would be difficult for his mother. The Henderson neighborhood was rougher than where Saul Jr. was attending school, and a mother naturally worries about her children. I wasn't concerned, of course, because I would be there with him, yet I wanted my queen peaceful and happy. Only if Saulito started indicating a strong desire to transfer to Henderson would Edna and I think seriously about such a move. Until then, the idea was on the shelf.

Another sacrifice both my wife and I make is balancing our personal life with commitments to the chess team. Training the team cuts into our personal and family time together. For me, that sacrifice for the good of the chess kids was worth it. But it was harder for Edna, because she and I have done everything together since we were 17 years old. When I am away for long periods of time when the team is traveling to tournaments, she is home without me. She is busy with work and with our kids, but when I'm on the road, or when I work late after school, and on Saturdays, it's a burden on her. It's a burden on me, too, because I miss her and our kids.

Mrs. Anzaldo was also sacrificing by leaving her kids when we went on the road or stayed late. It wasn't always easy for her and her husband to find people to watch their kids and take them to school when she was gone and he was at work.

Mr. Herrera's son's birthday happened to fall during our trip to the state tournament, and it was hard for him to be away; he's a very family-oriented man.

The decision to sacrifice isn't always easy. It's hard to exchange your queen for a rook, but if it will checkmate your opponent, it's worth it. The best we can do is calculate the benefits against the potential loss, and go for it.

The evening of the first day at State, we took the team to the Longhorn Steakhouse for dinner. They had never been to a restaurant that had cloth napkins on the tables.

After dinner, the kids went to their rooms and had a pillow fight to celebrate their successful day. Brandon and Pedro were pillow fighting on the bed, when suddenly Manny tackled Retana, and—CRASH—the support board broke and the bed folded like a hot tortilla. It was like the bad boys of chess had come to town to help a rock-n-roll band trash a hotel.

"What're we gonna do?!" Steven said.

The boys assessed the damage. The frame was broken but could be shored up. A little.

"We can fix it," José said. "I have a Gatorade bottle in my bag."

RULE 10: Sacrifice

José took a swig of Gatorade while the other three lifted the bed and he shored up what remained of the frame, balancing it just right on the bottle.

They all carefully stepped back.

"Better test it. Lightest person."

Chris gingerly laid on the bed and it began to lean and wobble. He slid off.

"Man, we better win tomorrow or we're in big trouble."

"Okay, nobody's sleeping on this bed tonight."

After a nervous chuckle about it all, the Henderson Chess Club intellectuals laid down on the floor next to the broken bed and drifted to sleep.

They had sacrificed a good night's sleep on a nice, soft bed during the most important tournament of their lives. But they had fun doing it.

The next day, after the fourth round, we weren't doing too badly, but we needed to kick it up just one more notch to really clinch the victory. I got them into a room and gave them a big motivational speech, making promises involving cotton candy, and generally pumping them up.

"Guys, we need a big round in the fifth, okay? You *really* need to step it up. Because there's nothing like going back to your hometown knowing you've lost."

"Alright, let's make it happen, Mister!"

Then one of them said, "What if it happens, Mister? We get pizza, right?"

They were negotiating with me. I liked their confidence.

I knew something was up when, in the fifth round, after they had been playing for nearly two straight days, most of our players were now playing against each other. That meant that Henderson had risen up the ranks, all the way to the top.

In chess, there's something called tempo. If you have the right tempo and the right timing, and you know how to execute a move, that's all that matters. Between the time when the team had gotten over their tough first round, and were about to enter the final round, Leo had settled into a very nice tempo and had won six out of six rounds. Brandon had won five out of six.

They were now playing the last round against each other, and both were playing well. Leo had tempo on his side, but Brandon had that indefinable something that could have given him a win against his teammate. That would have caused an interesting problem.

Brandon was a very quiet kid. He didn't speak English well, wasn't well off, and had a very interesting style. He was very close to his family in Juárez, and in his own way came across as "classy." But, the problem was, when I taught him in class, he never seemed to be paying attention. When I would explain to him what he should do, half the time he wouldn't even be looking at me. It seemed almost as if he didn't care. When he

RULE 10: Sacrifice

had first joined the team, I thought he wouldn't turn out to be a good player. I was wrong.

He was listening.

He was comprehending.

He knew what to do.

So, here was my problem: as he and Leo entered the final round, if Leo were to win the game, Brandon would drop to around fourth overall and that would drop the team into second place. But if Leo and Brandon were to draw, then Leo would get individual first place overall, Brandon would get second, and the team would win first place as a team. It was simple math, based on all the rounds that had been played, won, and lost. Leo had his first place in the bag, no matter what.

But he wanted to go undefeated at state in 2015.

I asked him to consider drawing.

"Play to a draw and you'll still get first place, Leo."

"But I can beat him, Mister."

"I know you can, Leo, but if you do, the team drops to second and nobody goes home with a first place but you. If you play to a draw, everyone goes home as winners."

"But I want to be undefeated, Mister. I can do it."

"No doubt, Leo. I know you can. What I'm asking you to consider doing is to sacrifice this one—not to lose, but just to draw, so the whole team can take winner trophies home."

He understood it, but his ego was fighting the concept of sacrificing in order to achieve something greater: a win for everyone on the team.

"This is all about teamwork, Leo. This is where teamwork comes in."

"But what if he comes in first and I come in second?"

"That's not going to happen because of all the other players' records. It's mathematically impossible."

He understood that, but he was resisting.

"I want to go 7-0."

"Please, Leo. Just draw. For the team. Please."

He and Brandon played...

It was a draw.

Seconds after the win, I sent a text to Mrs. Maldonado: *We have won state!*

After they were finished, while the other teams were still playing, I gathered the kids together, we got some chips and candy, and we went outside in the parking lot to celebrate with Freddie Mercury and Queen on our little speaker...

RULE 10: Sacrifice

Weeee are the champions, my friends!
And weeee'll keep on fiiighting 'til the end!
Weee are the champions
No time for loooosers!
'Cause we are the champions
...of the wooorld!

L-R:Lirio Gomez, Manny Tejada, Chris Carmona, Steven Mejia, Leo Gonzalez, Eduardo Retana, Brandon Caballero, Pedro Escobar, José Vanegas

Leo and Brandon immediately got a chessboard, went outside on the blacktop, and set up the pieces in the exact positions they were in when Leo asked for a draw.

They played.

The Champions' Game

Leo won.

He just needed to show that he could do it.

It was a lesson for Leo in being gracious and sacrificing one for the good of the team.

Music had always broken through with the kids, no matter how tired, or frustrated, or upset they were. Wherever we would go, they would have their speaker and their music. Before each round, they would listen to songs, dance, and have a good time—the chess party animals of Henderson Middle School. And Mrs. Anzaldo, Mr. Herrera, and I were having a good time right along with them.

Outside in the parking lot, Lirio walked over with her bag of chips as we started playing oldies from the 1960s.

Mr. Herrera grabbed her.

"C'mon, *mija*—let's dance!"

Shy little Lirio pleaded, "No!"

"Aw, come on—you're a champion!"

He tugged her over and she started dancing and having a good ol' time. It was the first time we had ever seen her relax and really join in the fun. And it wouldn't be the last.

RULE 10: Sacrifice

Soon, the whole team was cutting it up in the middle of the parking lot, dancing and having fun while everybody else was inside focused on finishing the tournament—which we had already won.

Leo, the 12-year-old sixth grader who had never played chess until the previous fall, won first place in the Middle School Novice Division in the entire state of Texas. Brandon was second. Lirio came in fourth. Chris was eleventh. Pedrito, twelfth. Retana, fourteenth. José was fifteenth. Steven, eighteenth. And Manny (whom I discovered only after the game was over had suffered a concussion playing football a few months earlier) came in twenty-sixth. He would soon become one of my top players.

Not bad, considering that most of them had first touched a chessboard no more than a year earlier.

I smiled at Lirio and said, "So, what happened?"

"Thank you, Mister," she grinned.

Out of seven rounds, she had won six, playing mostly against guys, and wound up in the top four—just as I had predicted before we had left El Paso for McAllen. The only round she had lost had been that first miserable one. And that was all in her head. She just needed permission to relax and have fun. Now she was.

"You see, *mija*?" I said. "You never know. It's not always about how you start or how much ahead you are in the game. It's how you finish the game that counts."

The Champions' Game

After we won, we invited Lirio's mom to come out and celebrate with us.

She politely declined, "No, this is Lirio's time."

"What?" I said. "Come on." Then I turned to Lirio and said, "Do you want your mom to come with us?"

"It doesn't matter, Mister. She can if she wants."

I felt a little awkward, because any other parent would've said, "Yeah! Let's go celebrate!"

She said, "No. It's fine. You guys go. This is Lirio's time."

She had learned when it was time to step back. She had a perfect balance of stepping up for her daughter and fighting for her when it was necessary, and pulling back when that was called for. She understood the need to let her daughter have her own time in her passion for chess.

Lirio really opened up at that state tournament. She had always been a very shy, introverted girl. During our drive to McAllen, she hadn't said more than a sentence or two. But by the time the team had won the championship, and we were singing and dancing in the parking lot, she had opened up. Mr. Herrera had even gotten her to dance.

As we were making the long, northwest, trek home, her mother said, "Wow! We've been trying to get her to open up for the last five years. And you guys did it in one little trip."

RULE 10: Sacrifice

The team members of the Henderson Chess Club had the time of their lives in McAllen. On the way home from their historic victory, we stopped in San Antonio and took the kids to the Alamo. As we were walking along the San Antonio River Walk, I thought about the past few years since I had become an art teacher at Henderson Middle School and had managed to deliver twice on my bold promise to Mrs. Maldonado.

I marveled at these kids, half of whom were English language learners, many of whom had never been outside of El Paso, never been to a fancy restaurant or eaten fast food (not that anyone could cook better than their *mamás* and *abuelas*), some who had never flown on a plane before, and nearly all of whom were from low-income families.

Most people probably wouldn't think of El Paso as the kind of place where these types of kids could be groomed into far above average chess players. But most people probably don't know El Paso. Criminologists say El Paso isn't safe *in spite* of its high proportion of immigrants, it's safe *because of them*. Studies have found that immigrants who come to America are less likely to commit crimes or to be incarcerated than native-born Americans. This is true for the nation as a whole, as well as for cities with large immigrant populations such as Los Angeles, New York, Chicago, and Miami, and cities along the U.S.-Mexico border like San Diego and El Paso.[3] This is also true for San Antonio, the bicultural city where the chess kids and I were leisurely strolling along the river, reveling in our victory.

[3] Reason.com in a July 6, 2009, story by Radley Balko titled, "The El Paso Miracle"; see: http://reason.com/archives/2009/07/06/the-el-paso-miracle

I have come to believe that I (or any good teacher) can take children from an impoverished neighborhood and turn them into champions. And not just at chess. My ultimate goal in my efforts with the chess clubs had always been to help the students earn college scholarships through mastering the intellectual game of chess, no matter what their personal, emotional, or economic situations.

Having won a state championship, the kids were now superstars. I knew that when we got home, the media attention would be intense.

RULE 10: Sacrifice

Chess had always been much more than just a game to me. After I had become Texas state champ in 2001, my coach and teacher David Romo had taken me to New York City so I could watch the national championship. There, I had experienced things I had never dreamed of doing, including staying at a five-star hotel.

Way back in middle school, I had first dreamed of one day becoming a teacher and taking a team of students to the national chess championship and watching them win first place. The 2015 National Junior High Championships were just a few weeks away in Louisville, Kentucky.

I was about to face my dream, I was thinking as we leisurely strolled along the River Walk.

But I was far more excited for the kids. Win or lose, they were about to go on the trip of their lives.

MS Novice	Sat-G/60 9 am	Sat-G/60 12:30 pm	Sat-G/60 3:30 pm	Sat-G/60 6:20 pm
MS JV	Sat-G/60 9 am	Sat-G/60 12:30 pm	Sat-G/60 3:30 pm	Sat-G/60 6:20 pm
MS Champ	Sat-G/60 9 am	Sat-G/60 12:30 pm		Sat-G/60 6:20 pm
				Sat-G/60 6:20 pm
Champ	Sat-G/60 9 am	Sat-G/60 12:30 pm	Sat-G/60 3:30 pm	Sat-G/60 6:20 pm

RULE 11

EXPECT THE UNEXPECTED

I always tell my students, when playing a game of chess, expect the unexpected. You can be playing your best, everything going your way, and then...BAM! You lose your queen.

Of all the unexpected things that could have happened at the tournament in McAllen, the biggest one was when I discovered some flaws in the way the championship was run. During the tournament, players from the same team are not supposed to play each other until the last round, no matter what the circumstances. But they had scheduled some of my team's play-

RULE 11: Expect the Unexpected

ers to face each other during earlier rounds, which was against the rules. At the time, I had not been aware of that rule. Had I known, the kids could've brought back first, second, third, fourth, fifth, sixth, seventh, and eighth places. All at that one tournament. We could have nearly swept state. All straight up and honest.

Afterward, when I realized what had happened, I thought, *That's crazy—these events are professionally run*! How could this happen? I was determined to make sure that sort of mistake didn't happen to my kids at the nationals.

But...*expect the unexpected*, right?

When we got back from McAllen, I knew there wasn't enough money to take the entire 12-member team to Kentucky for the nationals—which was going to be expensive—but that didn't matter. The kids did it. They had won the 2015 State Chess Championship.

My cousins, the Davids, had been playing chess since I had won the state championship in 2001. They were now attending UTEP and had heard about the Henderson state win. They volunteered to help with the team by playing against the kids, who needed good players to practice with. It would be good to have them around to help buffer the kids when the news media was at the school. Reporters were visiting almost every day, wanting to interview the team members.

The Champions' Game

Adrian Herrera and I went to the school office to speak with Mrs. Maldonado about the trip to nationals. I had my work cut out for me. Even with the team returning home as champions, it would be a battle to get funding in just eleven days to go to the nationals. For an economy trip to Kentucky I would have to come up with at least twenty grand. Maybe stay at Motel 6. Fly on an airline with two or three stops, eat peanuts for lunch, sit on the floor at the tournament.

Mrs. Maldonado told us that the school didn't have enough funds to send a larger group on a longer trip (one day more than state).

The cost would include:
– *me,*
– *a male chaperone, Mr. Herrera*
– *a female chaperone, Mrs. Anzaldo*
– *more hotel rooms and food,*
– *ground transportation,*
– *air travel more than twice as far*
  (all the way to Louisville, Kentucky).

"State already cost a lot," Mrs. Maldonado said, a little tense about the whole situation. "You want more to go to nationals? Fifteen people in all—three more than went to the state tournament?"

"That's too much," she said. "If you cut down on the team...I don't know. That still might be too expensive, because you would need to bring a chaperone. If you cut Lirio, you won't need a girl's chaperone."

RULE 11: Expect the Unexpected

"Cutting Lirio is not on the table," I said. "I already promised all the kids they could go to the nationals if the team won state. We won state."

"Maybe you shouldn't have made such a big promise."

"Big promise? The only girl on the team came in fourth in the entire state of Texas. How could we cut her out of the nationals team and hide something like that from the media?"

Tensions were high. The conversation was getting heated.

"Look, there's simply not enough money for everyone to go. Mr. Herrera is not going to be able to go. We can cut Mrs. Anzaldo too. At most, it's going to be you, and some of the kids. That's it."

"I'll pay for my own ticket. Mr. Herrera will take vacation time."

"That won't work. It still won't be enough."

"Okay, so *no* to Lirio, who just placed fourth in the entire state. No to Mrs. Anzaldo, who helped us so much at state that I couldn't even put a dollar figure on it. And no to my assistant coach, Mr. Herrera, who takes so much of the weight off of our shoulders and helps the kids with things from sunrise to midnight that it can't even be calculated. That's the deal?"

"You took nine kids to state. No need to take even more to the nationals."

I explained that it would basically be me, alone, dealing with all of the team's needs before the trip, during the flight to

Kentucky, all throughout the three days of the event itself, and traveling back to El Paso afterward.

"Mrs. Maldonado, I have been doing this for years. I know what it takes to prep, field, train, coach, and travel with a team to tournaments in a way that sets the kids up to win. And nationals are the most difficult of them all."

"We'll just have to make it work, won't we."

"Okay, then, we won't go to nationals," I responded.

I turned to go. Mr. Herrera looked at me as if I had just slapped the principal across the face.

Mrs. Maldonado looked at me like she hadn't quite heard what I had just said.

"*What?*" she said as I reached the door. "You're going to cancel the whole thing just because a few people can't go?"

She became extremely upset.

Mr. Herrera became very nervous.

I stood my ground.

"Yeah. But thanks for trying. I'll tell the kids it's all off."

I walked out. Mr. Herrera mumbled something apologetic to Mrs. Maldonado and hurried after me.

Mr. Herrera said, "Oh, man, that was harsh, bro. You better get your résumé ready. You're going to get fired now."

RULE 11: Expect the Unexpected

I thought, *¡Dios mío!, did I just do the wrong thing?*

It was tough but I had to stand my ground. The kids were worth the sacrifice. I was willing to walk away if the team wasn't set up to win.

Go big or go home.

A couple of days after my tense conversation with Mrs. Maldonado, she approached me and asked why I wanted Mr. Herrera to go to nationals.

I sensed the ice melting.

I told her, "Because he's my team's motivator. He's my right hand. He's there when I need him. The kids rely on him while I'm coaching and analyzing. Honestly? He's more important than a female chaperone—I know that's a requirement. But Mr. Herrera is a necessity. If he doesn't go, I don't go."

She sighed and said, "You know, you guys are right. Let's try fund raising again."

"*Gracias,*" I said.

It was a relief to know she had my back. I had been second-guessing myself nonstop since the hardball negotiating session, going back and forth, wondering if I was being wise or foolish.

But that was behind me. I had only two

Gracias–
thank you

weeks to raise at least $20,000 to take the entire team to the National Junior High Championships, which were being held during a three-day stretch from April 24 to April 26 in Louisville, Kentucky. Twenty grand was a lot of money for a community whose members averaged that much in take-home pay for an entire year. The only way we would be able to do it would be if the community came together and really went to bat for us.

We were about to find out what El Paso really thought of her children.

We calculated that we needed to raise at least $18,000 for a super low-budget trip. To do it right would cost around $25,000. So, we got busy.

Mrs. Maldonado wrote up a press release and sent it out to the school district's PR team. Those on social media reposted the press release and put it on their websites, saying that the kids were state champions and needed to raise money to take Texas to the nationals in chess. It went viral to all the newspapers and television shows.

It was a tsunami in the desert.

We scheduled a fund raising event that included a faculty-versus-student basketball game. We also let fans challenge Henderson players to a chess match in exchange for donations. We hustled like car window washers in Times Square for enough

RULE 11: Expect the Unexpected

money for us all to go—hopefully in style, the way I liked the kids to travel. After all, when most of them got out of El Paso, it was to go to Juárez. Not exactly a resort destination.

I wanted them to experience something completely different.

We put it out there to our UTEP alum that we needed help, and they came out for us in droves. So did many people from back when I used to play competitive chess. Even the woman who had steered me and Edna toward college a decade earlier showed up. She was now the new leader of the UTEP Talent Search program. This organization had always been very supportive of the kids in the El Paso community, and had really stepped up for at-risk kids like myself back then.

She asked me what we needed.

"Eighteen thousand dollars," I said.

"We'll pay for the hotel rooms."

That was $4,000 right off the bat.

The soil had already been tilled by the news frenzy, and people flooded the fundraiser events for eleven straight days. It was all over social media. It was everywhere. The El Paso County District Attorney came by, talked to the kids and mentioned the story. And then his associates came. How did these high-profile people all know about Henderson?

Decades earlier, the demographic of the area had been far more affluent. In the post-World War II era, when the G.I. Bill had made it possible for a family to purchase a nice house, the neighborhood around Henderson became a choice location to raise a family. Even parents who had lived in the projects sent their children over to Henderson Middle School to get a good secondary education. Many of these children had gone on to become people of influence in El Paso—district attorneys, state and federal judges, high-profile lawyers, F.B.I. agents, etc.

Henderson teachers started competing to see who could give more. It was like donation fever had swept through town. When one teacher would hear that another teacher gave $50, they would give $100. And when another teacher heard about that donation, they would give $200.

"You're single. You can give two hundred—Mrs. Rogers gave two hundred."

"Wait—Mrs. Rogers gave *two hundred?* I'll do three hundred!"

That was a lot of money for a teacher. And there were a lot of teachers kicking in. Mrs. Adame brought in $800 in donations from people she knew. Mr. Perez put in $200. Even Mrs. Torres, whose house our community service program had fixed up, came to the festivities and donated money to the cause.

A homeless man who the kids often saw near the campus came in one day to make a donation. He walked into the office saying, "This is for the chess club. I heard they needed the money."

Everyone was fighting hard for something that would benefit the kids and their futures, and in the process, it brought the community together. And I believe it brought people closer

RULE 11: Expect the Unexpected

to God. Parents, kids, everybody in the neighborhood around Henderson, and the entire community of El Paso came together. Without them, none of it could have happened.

We decided to hold a final fund raiser at Peter Piper Pizza (the restaurant agreed to donate 15 percent of the sales to the team). As the word got out, people arrived with donations. It was like the heavens lined up, and devils were shoved aside. Lawyers even came in with checks (*lawyers!—giving money away!*). One person had told another, and another one had told the next one, and it just exploded. It was a miracle, like a scene in a movie. The parking lot was full of beautiful automobiles, women in fur coats, and well-dressed movers and shakers. For days, the money kept pouring in. It was the first time in the school's history that the vault had to be used for money. Even news reporters who had gone to Henderson donated money.

By the time the drive was over, we had put in sixteen-hour days during eleven straight days of fund raising. Now all we had to do was count the money and see who was going to nationals.

The final tally was $11,000. Combined with the $4,000 UTEP would be paying for the hotel, we had $15,000. For a chess program that was only two years old, that wasn't bad. We were still $3,000 short of our target. But it would cost $25,000 to take the entire team to the nationals in style. For that we were $10,000 short.

And then, a math curriculum specialist from the University Interscholastic League (UIL) approached the principal.

The Champions' Game

The UIL is a large Texas organization that administers athletic, academic, and music contests for public primary and secondary schools. They had an offer to make us. They didn't have as many kids go into the UIL math team at state as they had anticipated and they had a little surplus cash left over. They wanted to give us some money. How much? $10,000.

Bam!—just like that, our entire ten grand shortfall was covered. Thank you God! The funds were transferred to the El Paso school district.

We were there. We had done it. Twenty-five grand and Kentucky here we come! Nationals, get ready for the Henderson Chess Club, two-time Texas state champs.

A lot was riding on my shoulders. And the whole community was watching. ♟

NEVER GIVE UP

I was taught by my chess coaches to play right up to the word "checkmate." Never quit. You never know what's around the corner. You never know what move or mistake your opponent might make that can give you an advantage. Don't quit, even when you think all is lost. And don't quit when you know you're doing the right thing.

For me, taking these kids to Kentucky was the right thing to do. They had earned it. Win or lose, it had been worth it not to compromise, nor to give up on my determination that they would *all* go to the tournament.

The Champions' Game

With the money challenge behind us, it was nice to finally be on the way with the kids to the airport to catch a plane for Kentucky. The fundraiser had been a huge lesson in never giving up, no matter what.

The National Chess Tournament started on a Friday, so I had to get the team to Kentucky on Thursday to check into the hotel, get them settled, and make sure they got plenty of rest the night before the competition began.

We arrived at the El Paso International Airport on Thursday in the early afternoon. As we waited in the terminal for our flight to be called, the kids were sitting on the floor, playing with their mobile phones, chattering excitedly, and looking out the windows at the airplanes on the tarmac. Ten of the kids would be flying for the first time in their lives.

Chris "Baby Face" Carmona was one of those ten. He was lounging on the floor with the others while clutching a little Bible scripture card his grandmother had given him, anxiously rubbing his fingers on it, reading it over and over again, muttering in anxious, silent prayer.

The others occasionally glanced at him with a mixture of pity and sympathy.

Pedro talked about having flown once before, to go to Iowa to visit family. René, who had been so pumped up to play chess at nationals that he had shaved the letter *H* (for Henderson) into the back of his hair, said he had flown to Cancún once.

But their talk wasn't doing much to calm Chris down. He was

RULE 12: Never Give Up

scared out of his wits. I prayed he wouldn't get another migraine from the stress.

Manny was having a rough time of it, too. He was shaking a little bit and had a worried look on his face. For whatever reason that kids do such things, two days earlier Manny had watched a movie starring Liam Neeson about a plane crashing. The next day—one day before our departure—he had become convinced that he was going to die in an airplane crash.

He had told his mom, "It's really stupid to fly! And I'm gonna get in an airplane tomorrow!"

"Calm down, *mijito*," she had said, and then joked, "You only have a fifty percent chance of dying."

"It's that high?!" he said.

She told him she was only joking, but between that and the movie the previous day, the image was set in Manny's fertile imagination.

Steven's mother, on the other hand, had told him that flying was really fun.

"You been watching too many movies and playing too many video games," Steven advised Manny.

"Planes crash in the news and stuff. It happens all the time," one of them threw in, confusing Manny and Chris all the more.

Chris started tearing up. He asked me, "Mister, what ocean are we flying over?"

mijito–
my dear son

"What do you mean *what ocean?*" I said. "We're going northeast to Kentucky, *mijo*. There are no oceans to fly over."

"Oh. Thank God."

Departure time arrived and they called our flight. Chris muttered something about missing his grandma and he started praying as we lined up.

We boarded the jet and got settled in. I glanced over at Chris. He looked so frightened, small, and frail, with his eyes as big as tea saucers.

The plane raced down the runway, lifted off, and banked into its flight vector and Chris cried out, "Oh my God!" and grabbed José's arm.

Manny burst out laughing, forgetting all about the Liam Neeson movie.

Chris screwed his eyes shut and mumbled under his breath, "Oh, man, oh, man! Oh my God, this is crazy! I don't wanna see this!"

Retana looked like he was about to cry.

Chris kept his eyes shut until we were in the sky. The others hung onto their seats like they were on a roller coaster that had reached the top of the steepest run and was about to race down the other side.

After leveling off at cruising altitude, the kids crammed next to the nearest window, slid open the shade, and became instantly mesmerized by the sight of white clouds all around us and patches of earth a few miles below us.

An excited smile crept to the corners of Chris' mouth, and I knew he would be okay.

The little champs were on their way.

I smiled and thought about my first flight to travel to a chess championship. Coincidentally, it was to go to the nationals, which were also held that year in Louisville, Kentucky. This was still with Mr. Medina and the high school team I was on when I had won the Texas state championship. First kid in my family to fly. First to win a state championship in anything. First to graduate from college.

When I had decided to go to UTEP and told everybody I was going to be an art teacher, they had all said I would never get a job. My mom had even said, "What is art going to offer your family?"

Then I had just one interview. One opportunity. And I did it. I had gotten it done in one shot. But I had always been a one-shot, never-give-up kind of guy. I had always asked God, "Just give me one opportunity and I'll do the work." I just need that one opportunity and I won't quit until I make it happen.

After we landed at the airport in Louisville, Kentucky, we went to pick up the vans.

Mrs. Anzaldo took the keys.

The Champions' Game

I held my hand out to her. "Give me the keys."

She shook her head, rolled her eyes, and gave me a look. "I know, I know. *Baaad luck* for women to drive at tournaments."

It had been a superstition of mine that started back in 2006 when my wife and I were in that horrible car crash while she was driving us home after my Segundo Barrio Chess Club lost badly at the nationals. Irrational response, sure. But every competitor had their lucky socks, weird routine, old baseball cap, rabbit's foot, whatever. Mine was probably weirder.

But I wasn't taking any chances.

The kids would have loved the experience of staying at a luxury hotel, but the one we wanted had been all booked up. We were on the waiting list and the odds of us getting rooms were slim to none, so we had reserved rooms at the Marriott. We were just glad to have made it to the tournament at all, after the battle we'd fought to get there.

Then I got a call from the Galt House, asking if we still wanted the rooms I didn't expect to get. I said yes! But I didn't tell the kids or Mrs. Anzaldo.

The Galt House is a beautiful, legendary, world-class, five-star luxury hotel on North Fourth Street in Louisville, Kentucky, where the 2015 U.S. Chess Federation National Junior High Chess Tournament was being held.

We arrived at the hotel around eight that night. It was a week or so before the Kentucky Derby and a lot of activity was happening in preparation for that event.

RULE 12: Never Give Up

I told the kids that this was where some of the top chess competitors were going to be staying and I just wanted to show them around before the tournament began the next day.

After we walked around the amazing, historic hotel, Mr. Herrera and I announced, "Alright, get your bags out of the vans."

"Huh? Why?"

"Because we're staying here."

"Noooo waaaay!"

Mrs. Anzaldo looked at me and said, "We're staying *here?*"

"Yep."

"No way!"

"Yep. We are. Surprise!"

"The whole time?"

"Whole time."

"...Noooo waaaay!"

Fun brings the kid out in everyone.

The hotel was divided in two parts, with twenty-four stories in one wing and nineteen in another, that were connected by a tunnel that went all the way to downtown Louisville and from there to the KFC Yum! Center. Right across the street from Louisville was the Ohio River, and across that was Indiana.

The Champions' Game

It didn't even matter if the kids won or lost at the competition over the next three days, they were already having the time of their lives.

And all Frankie was thinking about was bacon. The kid loved his bacon. He wanted to make sure he got bacon at the nationals.

Never give up, Frankie. ♜

Rook. Knight. Bishop. Queen. King. Bishop. Knight. Rook.

CONTROL YOUR CENTER

On a chessboard, you have to learn to control the four squares in the very center. Why control the center? Because ever thing goes through the center. It's a battleground. If you want to pass through to do anything, you have to go through the center. When a skyscraper is being created, where does the crane go? Right in the very center of the site, from where it can control the movement of material to and from every square foot of the site. Take a tree, for example. Trees are balanced at their very center, and even with all of the different sizes and lengths and weights of the branches, all trees are perfectly centered so they won't fall over.

The Champions' Game

Control the four center squares and you control the game.

I taught the kids that in the same way they need to control the center of the board, they needed to be in command of themselves. Your center is your spiritual life, your self-control. If you lose control, you lose yourself. That's why it's important to keep calm.

The first morning of competition, we got up early and had a little extra time, so we decided to take them to IHOP.

We mapped it out on the GPS, and Mr. Herrera and Mrs. Anzaldo and I discussed our options. The nearest IHOP was in Louisville, 2.7 miles away, and the directions had a lot of turns. But there was an even closer one, a straight drive just 2.1 miles away, over the bridge and across the state line in New Albany, Indiana. No-brainer.

We loaded the kids into the two vans and headed for the state line, with me driving the lead vehicle and Mr. Herrera behind me in the other.

It was a beautiful morning. The kids were jubilant. Spring was in the air.

It took us just a little bit longer to get to the IHOP than we thought it would, but we had plenty of time.

At the restaurant, the kids were in a great mood. We had a nice breakfast. Frankie ate all the bacon he could stuff in. Then we jumped in the vans and felt the tingle of excitement as we headed back to Louisville for the first round of the chess nationals.

RULE 13: Control Your Center

That's when we hit the traffic jam.

New rule: When you're at an important chess competition, never, ever, cross a state line or drive more than walking distance during early morning rush hour.

There was so much traffic that I started to panic as I tried to figure a way around it, knowing the clock was ticking down to start time. Then I remembered what had happened last year when I had taken the team to nationals. Some of our luggage never made it. We had to go to Wal-Mart to buy clothes for one of the students. And we got slaughtered. As if that memory wasn't bad enough, I flashed back to an even worse memory, the 2006 car crash—and that team had also gotten crushed at the national competition that year.

Oh, God! I thought. It's happening all over again. It was like a bad movie. Worse. It was a nightmare. The traffic wasn't budging. I was trying to control my center and not let the kids know my heart was pounding out of my chest while panic rose inside me. I was like a man trying to smile in front of a firing squad.

My cell phone rang. It was Mr. Herrera, in the van in front of me.

"What do we do, bro?" he said, his voice a mixture of amusement and worry.

I glanced in the rearview mirror. The kids in my van were starting to clamor about being late to their first nationals. Everyone was losing control of their center.

I said, "Dude, there's so much traffic...we're going to have to..."

"Bro, we need to get there."

"I know that, Adrian."

If you get to the nationals late, they don't care. If you arrive twenty minutes after the round, you lose the round, period. Plain and simple. No show, no go. And it tumbles like dominos from there, with one forfeiture following another, depending on how fast the games go and how much later you arrive.

I saw a sign up ahead that said DO NOT ENTER - EMERGENCY LANES ONLY.

As a chess champion, player, and coach, I don't recommend the course of action we were about to take. But, man, sometimes you gotta pivot!

Go big or go home!

I watched as Mr. Herrera's van suddenly shot into the emergency lane.

I muttered to myself, "I don't know where this guy's going, but..."

I hit the gas and stayed on his tail.

The kids started whooping, "Come on, Mister! We gotta get there first!"

May as well have been the Indy 500. It was crazy. I don't know how we did it, but we got there on time.

When we pulled into the parking lot, Mrs. Anzaldo stepped out of Mr. Herrera's van, walked over to me and held out her hand.

RULE 13: Control Your Center

"Give me your keys."

But at least Frankie got his bacon.

The nationals were nothing like the state tournament in McAllen, Texas. As the rounds began to get underway, the looks on the kids' faces said, *We're not in Texas anymore.* They looked intimidated as they got ready, once again, to play against kids who they definitely weren't used to seeing around El Paso. Black kids. White kids. Asian kids. Indian kids. Kids wearing fancy blazers. Kids wearing shirts and ties and jackets with emblems on them.

Our kids, on the other hand, were wearing scuffed up tennies and faded jeans that weren't made that way at the factory. Their shorts and frayed shirts had mismatched buttons. Kids from the barrio. Kids from Henderson Middle School. Texas state champion kids.

It was shaping up to be a different experience for them. It was like the land of the giants and a collection of unfamiliar cultures all rolled into one, staring down at them with a question in their eyes that seemed to say, "What are you doing here?" The kids were very intimidated. Their adrenaline was already racing from the mad freeway dash to get there in time. It took a lot of motivation and a lot of talking to get them to a place where they could relax a little.

"We are here to do what we do," I told them. "To play chess and to have fun. And if you bring home a win, that would be fun too. But it's not a requirement. You're here because you already earned it."

The national chess competition operated differently than the state tournament. The nationals were not closed-door. We could see the kids play from far away, but we could not see anything on their boards, which only created mystery since they all had poker faces and showed no emotions. This meant we wouldn't know what was going on at all until each player would emerge after the round was completed. It made for a mentally challenging experience for the kids and emotional times for us coaches and chaperones. We were dying to know what was happening. Were they having an easy time of it or not? Were they winning or losing? Were they having fun?

The minute they finished playing, we would see the whole story in their faces. You could be waiting by the door, all excited, then you'd see their expressions and that would dictate your own emotions the very next instant.

I had learned the hard way long ago that in the nationals, the other coaches won't talk to you. Not even small talk. To them, you were invisible. You could ask them something like, "Hey, how'd your girl do in that last round?" and what you'd get most of the time in response would be a stone wall of silence. Maybe a smile, but rarely. To be subjected to this could be very challenging if you tended to be a civil and polite person.

I saw a coach from another Texas team that wore fancy purple kangaroo jackets and, just trying to be friendly, I said to him,

RULE 13: Control Your Center

"Hey, how are you guys doing? You guys are also from Texas, right?"

His team had a lot of nice equipment. Nice chessboards, fancy pieces, cool clocks. We had our basic white pieces and four boards that I'd had since fifth grade.

The coach gave me a deadpan look for a second, then turned and walked away. Not a word. It was like I was seeing dead people and they didn't know they were dead.

Whoaaa, *hombre,* I thought. Chill, dude. I was only trying to be friendly. Of course, we had just taken first place from him in state and his was a team that had matching blazers and nice tables set up for them, while our butts were hurting from sitting on a hardwood floor in McAllen.

The kids started out well. René, our swag kid (whose grades had been too poor to allow him to go to state and had been replaced on that team by Manny) was determined to prove himself. He came out of the gate like a tiger. He won the first round.

"I'm going for first place, Mister," he told me.

"Wow—great job, René."

"You should've taken me to state."

"I wished we could have."

The Champions' Game

State had turned out fine; we won.

But what was unfolding at nationals was a disaster.

When Frankie walked into the competition hall, he was surprised by the sheer size of it. It was the biggest room he'd ever been in. You could park a plane in there. His first match was with a kid from New York who surprised Frankie when he spoke a little bit of Spanish. Frankie had thought that the kids from El Paso were the only ones there who spoke Spanish. His guard went down just a little bit.

And he lost his very first round.

Retana started off well. He won his first match.

Retana emerged from the round and said out loud, "Mister! I kicked his ass!"

"Retanaaa," I said, "Don't say that."

And that's when I started seeing cracks appear in the team. He was such a quiet kid in the classroom—my isolated pawn—that you would never know he had such exuberance in him.

"Don't say that!" I shushed him as I quickly guided him away from the open area. "Don't...don't say anything, *mijo*. Okay?"

Then he started speaking in Spanish in kind of a singsong pattern, like the *narco corridos* he idolized.

"Retana," I said sternly, "this is a gentleman's game. You do not behave that way. You gotta learn to be just as gracious in victory as you are in loss."

RULE 13: Control Your Center

"Yeah, but Mister, he knows I kicked his ass."

¡Ay, Dios mío! His humble was so gone.

Leo was struggling with modesty, too. He had just come off of winning first place at state, and by the time the nationals were underway, his ego was flying.

"I'm the best!" he bragged.

"Leo," I told him, "you need to humble down, boy. You remember what I told you? You can't be too excited. And right now, you're too excited."

"Don't worry, I've got this, Mr. Ramirez," he said confidently.

Sure enough, as soon as he walked out of the round, it was written all over his face: he had lost—in his very first round.

"What happened?"

"I lost, Mister."

It was the humbling of Leo. He came up to me, head hanging, eyes watering.

"Mister, I let you down."

"Yes. You sure did. But remember what I told you when we got here?"

"Yes, Mister. I'm sorry. But I've beaten this kid before."

"I know, Leo. But this is different. Now he wants to beat you too. So shake it off, focus, and do better next round."

The Champions' Game

The worst thing about it was that Leo said he knew what he did wrong. He had been setting the kid up, but he'd made a mistake in the setup and the kid had caught it. And, boom, he took the Texas state champ to school.

But it wasn't over yet.

"You learned your lesson, right?"

"Yes, Mister."

"It's time to come back up. You gotta bring your ego down, bring your game up, and get your humble on."

"Yes, Mister."

He dried his eyes, shook it off, and said, "It's alright. I'm going to get him tomorrow, Mister."

And then, before I could get the kids settled down and get their emotions under control, Lirio had a meltdown.

Lirio had cried for the first time at state. Now she was crying again at nationals. She lost her first round pretty badly and the waterworks started. She ran all the way to her room, wailing like a fire truck. She was done, she didn't want to play the next round because she was afraid it was going to happen again and she would cause the team to lose.

Her emotions were flaring. With her mother, her sister, and Mrs. Anzaldo there in the room with her, she cried out, "*¡Sólo quiero hablar con Mr. Herrera!*"

¡Sólo quiero hablar con Mr. Herrera!– I only want to talk to Mr. Herrera! ✱

RULE 13: Control Your Center

She wanted to talk to Mr. Herrera and Mr. Herrera only.

"Mamá, no quiero hablar contigo. ¡Salte por favor!"

She kicked her mom out of the room and demanded they send up Mr. Herrera.

I was downstairs with Adrian, waiting for Lirio to get it together and return to the competition when my phone rang. It was Mrs. Anzaldo.

She said, "She won't come down."

"She what?" I said. "We have a game to play here."

"She wants to talk to Mr. Herrera only."

"What's going on with her?"

"She's upset, Saul. She's a teenage girl, the only girl on the team, she just lost a round, she feels like she's letting everyone down, she—"

"I get it, I get it. We'll be right up."

I clicked off the call, turned to Mr. Herrera, said, "Let's go. She won't come out of her room."

In a reversal of his usual image as the school disciplinarian, the chess kids had come to see Mr. Herrera as a big, burly, cuddly, protective big brother. So it made

Mamá, no quiero hablar contigo. ¡Salte por favor!– Mom, I don't want to talk to you, just go! PLEASE! ✱

sense that during times like these, Lirio would be more in need of his *wassup, girl?*-style than my no-nonsense *Lirio, why are you acting this way?*-approach.

We got upstairs to her suite and heard the sound of an emotional outburst coming from Lirio in her bedroom just as her mother, sister, and Mrs. Anzaldo were backing quickly out of the room.

Mrs. Anzaldo pulled the door closed and said to Mr. Herrera, "She wants to talk to you only."

I told him, "Go in and talk her down, bro."

He looked at me. He looked at the closed door from where the emotional outburst had come. He looked at Mrs. Anzaldo.

He said, "Uhhh...you know what? Let's send Mrs. Anzaldo in there," as if we'd asked him to go in and conduct an exorcism.

Mrs. Anzaldo said, "She wants you. She kicked her mom and sister out. She said Mr. Herrera only."

"Go in and talk to her," I said. "See if you can calm her down."

"But I'm supposed to be the mean one. The disciplinarian."

"She's losing control and we need her to get her head back in the game. Go."

He gingerly opened the door a crack and announced timidly, "*Mija?* You okay in there?"

Go! I mouthed and nodded toward the door.

RULE 13: Control Your Center

He nodded back and disappeared reluctantly into the room. The door closed behind him.

I looked at my watch. Time was ticking down and I had an emotional teenage girl on my hands whose chess ability I badly needed back on the team. Right now. I did not want these hard-working kids to return to El Paso without a big trophy to show off, not after all we'd gone through to get here.

But this could be a tricky negotiation. Here was this little girl, 13 years old, eighth grade, last year in middle school and headed for high school in less than six months, first time at the nationals, hormones and pressure and frustration all over the place, only girl on the team, everybody counting on her...and probably all she wanted right then was the father she used to play chess with years ago.

In the bedroom, Lirio was completely under the covers. Mr. Herrera eased down onto the edge of her bed and said to the lump of blankets, "Hey, Lirio! *¿Qué te pasa, calabaza?* It's me, Mr. Herrera."

No response.

"Lirio, either way, if you play anymore or not, no matter what, you know, you're still a winner."

Slight movement under the blanket.

"You can do whatever you want. Nobody's pressuring you to do anything. Ok? Not while I'm around, *mija.*"

Slowly the covers drew down, exposing her head.

"Thank you," she said in a small voice, dragging a sleeve across her wet cheeks.

"Hey," he grinned, "that's more like it."

A smile peeked out from the corners of her mouth.

Mr. Herrera asked, "You know where Mr. Ramirez wants to go?"

"Where?"

"KFC. Maybe McDonald's. You wanna go to the Yum Center? It's right here in Louisville."

"What's that?"

"Uh...I don't know—it's the KFC place!...Lirio, what's the problem? Why are you scared? What's wrong?"

"I lost and I let you guys down."

"Say *whaaat?* What're you talking about? Look where we're at! Look out the window at this great view! You got a suite here that's so big you can kick people out and they're still in. You know what I mean?"

She giggled.

"Look how far we've come, *mija*. Look what we've done."

She nodded and said, "I don't want to let them down."

"You didn't let anybody down. It's chess! Everybody's up and down. You're part of the team. That's what counts, right?"

RULE 13: Control Your Center

She stuck a foot out from under the blanket. He tickled it. She laughed.

"You better put your shoes on or I'ma tickle you even worse!"

"Okay! Okay!" she giggled.

"Come on, let's go eat."

Lirio lost control of her center. Mr. Herrera helped her find it.

Today, it seemed like every one of them was needing some help.

Some more than others.

It was obvious we all needed to get out during the next break. So we decided to take the kids on a walk to get sandwiches at Subway, which was eight blocks away.

We sent them to their rooms to get ready. Twenty minutes later we knocked on their doors and they came out, each with their assigned partner, ready to go.

We started walking. With a dozen kids, it would be a thirty-minute walk. It was a nice day. Weather was fine. At two or three blocks out, Mr. Herrera did the head count.

"We're missing one," he said.

"Can't be possible. Count again."

He did. We were one kid short of a team.

"How is that possible?" Mrs. Anzaldo asked. "We took them all out of the room."

"Who's missing a partner?!"

"René, where's your partner—where's Frankie?"

"Oh, dang, Mr. Ramirez. He's not here!"

"I know he's not here! Where is he?!"

"I don't know where I left him, Mister."

"What do you mean you *don't know where you left him*?! How could you lose Frankie!?"

I felt panic rising in me.

It wasn't René's fault, of course. We all just got caught up in the activity of getting ready to go, and when the big group left, we thought we were all there. Twelve kids and three adults is a big crowd. A person could get lost. Shouldn't. But could. And did.

While we were frantically trying to figure out how and where we'd lost Frankie, I got a call from the hotel.

"Mr. Ramirez, we have one of your players here at the front office."

"Oh, thank God."

He put Frankie on the phone.

"I'm sorry I wandered off, Mister," he said. "I went to go play with the New York kids."

RULE 13: Control Your Center

I ran back to the hotel and when I arrived, there he was, playing chess with the New York kids.

This was nothing new for Frankie. One thing about Frankie was that he would always walk a little behind us when we would walk to lunch or wherever. He also seemed to have more fun meeting other people than he did socializing with his own team. He would occasionally wander off to talk to other kids at the tournament and forget that he was part of our team. That tendency seemed to get worse as his level of play began to waver between highs and lows.

His center was all over the place, in a different way than Lirio's. He was a gifted student but there was a lot of heaviness on that little boy's heart and mind. More than a 12-year-old child should have.

All I could think was, *why are we having such a tough time of it here at the nationals?*

Right now, they weren't winning, because none of them were focusing. To make any of the rules work, their full attention and intellectual capacity had to be focused on the game.

But children can be pretty emotional, and that throws off their focus. Lirio, for example, had started playing chess when she was in sixth grade. She was very smart. In fact, when she had first joined the team, I knew right away how intelligent she was by how quickly she grasped advanced chess concepts. But she often let her emotional state interfere with her focus. And if she didn't get control of her emotions, it could be her downfall.

The Champions' Game

We came back from Subway, and the kids continued playing. The team was not doing well at all. At first they were down, then they were up, then the next round they came back down, then they'd go up to second, then to first, then third, then first again. They were up and down like a pogo stick. We might as well have been on a roller coaster at Six Flags.

I started feeling sick and feverish.

"Don't stress out," Mrs. Anzaldo said.

The last time I got sick at a major tournament, we lost. Bad.

Oh, I was stressed alright.

"We all want to come back with first place," Mr. Herrera said.

"It's not whether we want to, bro, we have to come back with first place. We have to."

I was stressing as much as the kids were.

RULE 13: Control Your Center

By the end of the fifth round, we were in second place, but it was coming down to the end and we could easily sink to third. And I wasn't going to let them go back to Henderson with a third-place anything. I was upset with myself, upset with the team, upset with everything.

The day was over. Tomorrow I had a big task ahead of me: I had to both pump them up and settle myself down. We all needed to find our centers.

VISUALIZE YOUR WIN

In chess, you have to visualize your end game. Throughout the game, your focus is checkmate. But it's about more than just having a purpose. You need to see in your mind your goal becoming a reality.

We were there to play competitive chess, which required serious focus. And that had been seriously lacking. Something had to change.

I did not want to see them lose.

Our hometown came together in such a big way to pay for this trip, to get these twelve kids to the nationals in Kentucky. There was no way I was going to allow us to let down our community, or El Paso.

RULE 14: Visualize Your Win

Part of the problem was that the kids were overly distracted. The hotel was huge and magnificent. It was like three hotels in one. It was humongous. On that first day, when each of our team members would finish a round, they would come out of the tournament room and say, "I'm finished. Can I go look around the hotel?" We'd say, "Yeah, sure. Go have fun."

And while we were analyzing their games, they would be wandering around the hotel, goofing off, exploring. They weren't focused. They weren't learning. There were just running all over the place, enjoying the experience of a luxury hotel for the first time in their lives. Going up and down in the elevators. Playing like crazy. Not focused. As a result, they had not been playing at their best. It was a miracle we were in second place at that point. But with how erratically they'd been playing, that could go down...fast.

I had to get them straightened out. We were there to have fun, sure. But not to play around. That part could come after they earned it. Right now, they were there to compete.

"What should we do?" Mr. Herrera asked.

Whenever you're in trouble, go back to basics.

"Let's take it old school. Let's do like we did at state. Let's put them together in a room and talk to them, remind them who they are. The same as we did at state."

Herrera and I called the twelve into the room.

"Alright kids," I said, "everybody close your eyes."

They closed their eyes.

"I want you to just relax and think about our goal. Think about why you guys came over here. We played so many practice games, played so many little tournaments. We went to state and won. Flew so many miles to be here. Think about all of that. Think about why we are here."

I let that sink in for a few moments.

"Right now, you guys are doing terribly. But that's ok. You made some mistakes. Let's move on. Who are you guys?"

"I'm Leo, Mister."

"I know you're Leo. But who y'all are is state champs. You are the best of Texas. And Texas is one of the biggest states in the United States. It's bigger than New York. It's bigger than Florida. It's much bigger than Kentucky. You guys are the champions in Texas. All of your points count. Everything counts. Just you being here counts. But right now, we're behind. And we need to catch up. So I want you to close your eyes and just sit quiet and still for two minutes and see yourselves grabbing that first-place trophy. Visualize it."

I waited a moment.

"Does anybody see themselves getting a first-place individual trophy?"

No one raised their hand. I didn't say anything.

"Just keep on visualizing. Who wants second place? Who wants third? Whatever you are visualizing right now, that's what you're going to get."

RULE 14: Visualize Your Win

I kept on going like that for fifteen minutes, encouraging them to visualize their win.

"What did we come here for?"

"To win, Mister!"

"Exactly. And right now, you guys are not doing that. So, again, I want you to visualize, just like in the game of chess. Picture yourselves getting that first-place trophy. Can you see it?"

They became very quiet and said nothing.

"Exactly," I said. "You can't see it. Because it's not happening. It's slipping through. But you've paid your dues to be here. Yeah, you've made a few mistakes, but you'll pull through. So just remember who you are and decide that you're not gonna lose."

And I let Freddie Mercury take it from there...

> *Weeee are the champions, my friends!*
> *And weeee'll keep on fiiighting 'til the end!*
> *Weee are the champions*
> *No time for loooosers!*
> *'Cause we are the champions*
> *...of the world!*

The kids rocked the house and started belting it out with Queen at the top of their lungs.

"This is who you are!" I said over the cacophony. When the song finished playing, I said, "You guys are the champions! You beat every other team in the ENTIRE state of Texas! Now who are you?!"

"Champions!"

"Didn't quite hear that!"

"CHAMPIONS!"

"That's right. You're not here by accident. You're here because you belong here. You want to be national champions as a team? Let's make it happen."

"Yes, Mister!"

"Now go to your rooms and take a nap. I'll wake you up. Then we'll go eat and we'll keep on playing."

I had done all I could.

Mr. Ramirez, Mrs. Anzaldo, and I took a walk to get our focus together, too.

When we got back, we took them to get something to eat.

When we returned to the tournament, I told the kids, "Mrs. Anzaldo, Mr. Herrera, and I are going to be sitting right here by this door, waiting for you. After this round, as soon as you're finished and you walk out, you come over here. And you sit with us."

Playtime was over. It was time to get serious.

After that, they started doing really well. Their emotions were changed. They were behaving like professionals. They were focused. As they came out of the room, they gave us the play-by-play and went over their games instead of running off to explore.

They wanted this win.

But it wasn't going to come easy.

Manny Tejada was concerned about the skill of a kid he hadn't played since state but who was cleaning up the nationals.

Manny said, "Mack Macy's name will give me nightmares forever—he won almost every single round!"

For Steven, it was a kid named Carson. "That guy destroyed me!"

Chris said, "I played Carson last round, and he beat me. It really was hard. He played five out of our seven players, and he beat all of them."

Leo chimed in, "I lost to him in state, then I beat him bad today."

"I'm up next against one of the girls from that team with the kangaroo shirts," added José.

Mr. Herrera, Mrs. Anzaldo, and I recalculated all the numbers. I could barely believe what I was seeing on the sheet, while my hands were shaking with nervousness.

"José...if you beat her, that's it. We win."

It had all come down to that final round.

José, who was near the bottom in points.

The Champions' Game

And the girl with the kangaroo shirt, who was in third.

They were behind those doors, going head-to-head.

If near-last-place José (who was one of five children being raised by a hard-working mother in a family with no dad around) were to beat number three kangaroo girl, our total would add up to 16 and a half points. And the next highest team would total 16. But José hadn't been performing well at all. Since we couldn't watch the action at the nationals, I had no idea what was going on behind those closed doors. Did José, a seventh grader from an impoverished Juárez family, have it in him to beat the girl who had been stepping on our toes the entire tournament in her fancy team jacket? Remember, this was the same José who was inconsistent. Up one day; crash and burn the next.

I let out a breath, my mind refusing to let go of recalculating the numbers over and over again. There was zero margin for error. He wins, we go home as champs. He loses, we go down in flames.

José came out of the room. His face told it all.

He was grinning from ear-to-ear.

"I won, Mister! I made her my—"

"DON'T SAY IT!"

We were so excited we could barely stand it.

He had just kicked a game-winning field goal in the last few seconds of the last quarter of a tournament that could have gone either way.

RULE 14: Visualize Your Win

José Vanegas, Pedro Escobar, Joshua Valero, Lirio Gomez, Eduardo Retana, Manny Tejada, Chris Carmona, Steven Mejia, Leo Gonzalez, Brandon Caballero. Front Row: Frankie Marquez, René Rodriguez

I recalled the year before, when I had taken the 2014 team to the nationals and we had gotten creamed—19th place—and as I had been sitting there in disbelief, I had said to myself, "Next year I am coming back and winning this."

And we did.

But the most beautiful thing about the win was that we had played as a team. Even though we only had one kid place in the top ten, they had each played strong as a team. We might have known who our more consistent players were, but we also knew that on any given day, any one of our team members could show up and play at top level.

You don't fight your battles alone.

Leo wound up ranking the highest on the team and took 6th place individually in the nation (and instantly became a nationally-ranked player). Brandon placed 13th nationally, Chris 14th, René 15th, Pedro 17th, Retana 18th, José 19th, Lirio 24th, Steven 27th, Manny 40th, Frankie 41st, and even Josh (who had been playing football, basketball and soccer) at 48th place, drew two games and got one point to contribute to our narrow win. Everyone contributed.

And the team itself took first place in their division in the entire nation.
Not bad for a weekend's work.

As was our "custom," we decided not to wait for the official announcement while the other teams finished. We knew we had it in the bag, so even before the official announcement of our win, we went out to celebrate. I usually waited until after the ceremony to take the kids out to dinner, but we had a dozen hungry champions on our hands and the The Old Spaghetti Factory awaited (the kids had never been to one).

It was time to relax and have fun. The battle was won.

RULE 14: Visualize Your Win

After we got back to the hotel from the The Old Spaghetti Factory, Mrs. Anzaldo, Mr. Herrera, and I sat in my room and discussed the weekend's events while the kids had fun in one of their rooms. And boy did they have fun. So much so that Corporal Brown had to show up to calm the party down.

Our floor had already emptied out because most of the contestants, their entourages, and chaperones had checked out after the tournament celebration was over, but we stayed an extra day.

As the evening wore on, we decided to go out and buy the kids some dinner.

We told them, "You guys can have a ball. We're gonna go out and get you some chicken wings and we'll be right back."

When we got back with the wings and entered their room, Steven was seated in a swivel chair being spun around by Chris and René at high velocity.

They all froze the instant they saw us.

"What are you guys doing?" I said.

"Sorry, Mister. We're just playing."

"You did say have a ball...You want to try it?"

My mind raced for a second.

They're just having fun. They're just kids. They're the national chess champions.

"Okay. Just once. But don't wreck the furniture."

"YAY!"

I sat down and let them spin me around a couple of times, and managed not to throw up.

Then they said, "Now it's Mr. Herrera's turn!" and they spun him...as best they could a former pro-football player who tipped the scales at over 250.

"Now it's Mrs. Anzaldo's turn!"

Being a bit small, Mrs. Anzaldo didn't weigh as much, so they gave her a good hard spin—and she went flying out of the chair and got a bruise on her leg.

We gave them the chicken wings, told them to tone down the noise and rowdiness, and not to wreck the hotel room. We then went back to my room for some peace and quiet.

After a few minutes, we could hear their commotion from two doors down.

"You know," I said, "if we can hear them from here, we better calm them down."

Mr. Herrera got on the hotel phone and called their room.

"Hey you guys, you need to calm down. You're getting a little loud. Someone is going to complain, okay?"

They said, "Sure. We'll chill out."

RULE 14: Visualize Your Win

It was quiet for ten minutes, then they were back up to full volume.

"Should we start calling it quits?" Mrs. Anzaldo said.

I said, "Naw, let's give them a little bit more time."

Mr. Herrera said, "Hey...let's have a little fun with them," and he picked up the house phone and dialed their room.

He put on his best female voice. "Hello? Yes, this is the front desk. You need to calm down or I'm going to have to call your chaperones. Is there an adult there who I can speak with?"

Sure enough, a couple of them came running down to my room.

"Mr. Ramirez, Mr. Ramirez, they called us from the front office!"

I went down to the room with them. They handed me the phone.

"Yes?" I said to Mr. Herrera, who was on the line from my room. "...Yes, ma'am, I'm the chaperone, Mr. Ramirez. ...Yes, I'm so sorry, ma'am. ...Okay, I'll have them quiet down."

I hung up the phone and told the kids, "You guys are making too much noise. That lady was really upset. You gotta stop and go to bed now."

"No, Mister! Please, just a little bit longer. We'll stay quiet, we promise! We're gonna play chess now, okay? Please?"

"Hmmm...alright. But just a little while."

"Thank youuuu!"

I went back to my room and the three adults had a little chuckle and continued talking.

Less than half an hour later, the volume was back up to full throttle from down the hall.

That's when Corporal Brown made his appearance.

Mr. Herrera got on the phone, called the kids' room and put on his best Southern cop drawl.

Leo answered.

Mr. Herrera said, "This here's Corporal Brown from the Loo-ville po-leece department. Please be advised that we now have a patrol unit headed to your location due to reports of a public disturbance."

Mrs. Anzaldo clapped a hand over her mouth and started laughing so hard she rolled off of her chair.

"Corporal Brown" Mr. Herrera continued with Leo. "I need to talk to an adult right now, young man."

"Yes, Sir."

Leo shoved the phone at Pedrito, said, "Talk to him! I gotta go get Mister!" and bolted out the door.

We heard the pattering of kids' feet running down the hallway. I looked out the peephole and saw Lirio scamper into her room and quietly close the door.

There was a knock on my door. Herrera clamped a hand over the

RULE 14: Visualize Your Win

phone's mouthpiece.

I casually opened the door. Leo was standing there, his eyes wide with fright.

"Hey, Leo. What's going on?"

"The police are coming!"

"The what?"

"The police! We told them we won a national championship and we were just having a little fun celebrating. We're not doing anything bad, Mister! You need to talk to them, please! They're sending a police car here right now!"

"Ohhh, no! You guys..."

I turned to Mr. Herrera and said, "I'm going down to their room to see what's going on." I hurried to the door, then stopped, turned back to him and added in a worried tone, "Hey, if they take me to jail tonight, make sure you bail me out, okay, bro?"

"Yeah, okay!"

I headed out the door with Leo. We rushed down the hallway to the room.

Pedro was on the phone with "Corporal Brown."

"So, what's your name, son?" he was saying on the phone to Pedro.

"Pedro Escobar, sir."

"Escobar? You mean like the drug dealer kingpin guy from down in Juárez? That Escobar?"

"No, no, I'm not related—I don't do—yes, it's the same name, but I'm not a, I don't—"

"How old are you, Pedro?"

"Eleven, Sir."

"Okay, Pedro, I'm gonna be over there in two minutes with the dogs and cuffs. You stay put and don't go anywhere."

Herrera hung up.

I entered the room. Pedro looked like he was going to faint. Chris was terrified, his face completely drained of color.

"Guys, what happened here, what's going on?!"

Pedro answered, "Mister, the cops are coming and we're goin' to jail!"

Brandon said, "They can't take me to jail, can they?—I'm only twelve!"

Leo was standing behind me, muttering, "Oh my god, this can't be happening. Oh my god, oh my god!—they're gonna take my trophy away!"

Mr. Herrera treaded in and said, "Was that Corporal Brown from the Louisville Police Department on the phone?"

"Yes, Mister!" Pedro cried out. "And he was..." He suddenly stopped talking as I started to crack up laughing.

RULE 14: Visualize Your Win

Mrs. Anzaldo appeared in the doorway, giggling so hard she was doubled over, holding her stomach.

I burst out laughing.

Leo and Pedro looked at us with puzzled faces, trying to analyze what was going on.

Mr, Herrera continued, "Did he sound like this here: How y'all doin'? I'm Corporal Brown from the Loo-ville po-leece department."

Suddenly, the familiar accent dawned on them.

Pedro wagged his head sadly and said, "Man...that's messed up."

Herrera laughed and said, "Aw, man—we were just joking!"

Leo asked, "Does this mean we're not going to jail?"

Chris said accusingly, "Why would you do that to us? We're just kids!"

We were still chuckling as we walked out and went down to Lirio's room. We knocked on her door.

After a few minutes, she opened the door and stood there faking a yawn and rubbing her eyes as if she'd been in deep REM sleep for hours.

"I've been sleeping. Why'd you guys wake me up?"

Yeah, right!

Even big kids like to have a little fun in life.

The Champions' Game

The kids might not tell you they had fun with Corporal Brown after they won the nationals, but the real fun started for them the minute we arrived at the airport to head home to Texas, because we made a point to walk into the terminal holding the trophies high so everybody would see them.

People wanted to know what the trophies were for.

"These kids are from El Paso," I explained proudly. "They just won the national championship title in chess."

On the plane, the captain announced over the speakers, "Ladies and gentlemen, this is the captain speaking. We want to congratulate the National Championship chess team from Henderson Middle School in El Paso, Texas, who are flying with us today."

Everybody started clapping. The kids loved it.

When we arrived at the El Paso airport, we were greeted with balloons, cheering crowds, clapping, chanting, yelling...and TV news crews.

We were the champions. And the champions were home.

RULE 14: Visualize Your Win

HENDERSON MIDDLE SCHOOL CHESS TEAM BRINGS HOME NATIONAL TITLE

El Paso's Henderson Middle School chess team won the National Junior High Championship novice division this past weekend...

"After winning state, this year's team ran into another challenge: raising enough money to pay to take all 12 players to Kentucky. ...The Hornets launched an online fund raiser and held events to raise the $18,000 they needed to pay for the trip. ...'It was a lot of money we had to put together in such a short time,' [the team's Coach, Saul] Ramirez said. 'The only way that was possible was the community came together.'

"The team from South-Central El Paso kept a small but steady lead throughout the tournament, beating a Miami private college preparatory school, Gulliver Schools, by one point. ...the team is the first from El Paso to win the title.

"More than 96 percent of Henderson students are from low-income families. A third are English Language Learners."

- *El Paso Times*[4]

[4] *El Paso Times*, in a May 28, 2015, story by Lindsey Anderson titled, "Henderson Middle School chess team brings home national title."

EPILOGUE

THE NEW KINGS AND QUEENS

At this point you probably have a few questions. If you're a teacher, you might be wondering how their victory affected their success in school? If you're a chess player, you might be wondering what specific moves they used to win? If you're a kid, you might be wondering what happened to Lirio, Retana, Manny, and the rest of the team after the championship? If you're from El Paso, you might be wondering why the star at the top of the Franklin Mountains was lit up in their honor? Not even U. S. Presidents got the star lit up in their honor.

There are no simple answers to these questions. Instead, I'd like to paint a picture for you.

Henderson Middle School Homecoming.

2015.

Lights are dim.

Music is jammin'.

Students are dressed to impress.

NOW ... look over to the middle of the dance floor, there surrounded by their friends and all of the cheerleaders...
                    the chess team.

Mrs. Maldonado takes the mic. Everyone gets quiet. She smiles.

EPILOGUE

"Students, last week y'all got on your iPads and voted for your Homecoming Court.

Here they are..."

You might be picturing a court filled with football players and cheerleaders. You might be picturing a few volleyball players in there too.

But not this year.

This year, most of the court was the chess team.

The chess kids are the cool kids.

The new kings and queens.

Left to right: Erika Martinez–8th grade Queen (cheerleader), Pedro Cuellar–8th grade King (chess player), Mia Martinez–7th grade Princess (chess Player/volleyball player) Saul Ramirez–7th grade Prince (chess player) Roxxane Enriquez–6th grade Duchess (chess player), Devonte Aguirre–6th grade Duke (chess player)

APPENDIX

A few weeks after our win, the state of Texas House of Representatives issued a Resolution signed by four county commissioners and a county judge for the kids' accomplishments...

The State of Texas
House of Representatives

H.R. No. 2832

RESOLUTION

WHEREAS, The chess team from Henderson Middle School in El Paso took top honors in its division at the United States Chess Federation National Junior High Championship in April 2015; and

WHEREAS, Competing in the middle school novice category at the Galt House in Louisville, Kentucky, the team received important contributions from each player as they outmaneuvered their foes to claim the first-place trophy; with the victory, the Henderson chess team became the first squad from an El Paso school to win a USCF national title; and

WHEREAS, Henderson was led by Leo Gonzalez, who finished in sixth place, and he was joined in the top 20 by Brandon Caballero in 13th place, Chris Carmona in 14th place, Rene Rodriguez in 15th place, Pedro Escobar in 17th place, Eduardo Retana in 18th place, and Jose Vanegas in 19th place; also contributing to the championship triumph were Lirio Gomez, Steven Mejia, Manny Tejada, Francisco Marquez, and Joshua Valero; moreover, each student benefited greatly throughout the year from guidance provided by HMS chess coach Saul Ramirez; and

WHEREAS, With their accomplishments at the National Junior High Championship, the members of the Henderson Middle School chess team proudly represented their school, and the dedication the students have demonstrated is sure to serve them well in the years ahead; now, therefore, be it

RESOLVED, That the House of Representatives of the 84th Texas Legislature hereby congratulate the Henderson Middle School chess team on winning the novice division at the United States Chess Federation 2015 National Junior High Championship and extend to its members and coach sincere best wishes for the future; and, be it further

RESOLVED, That an official copy of this resolution be prepared for the team as an expression of high regard by the Texas House of Representatives.

Blanco

APPENDIX

And the media attention continued throughout the year...

66 HENDERSON CHESS TEAM CONTINUES ITS MOMENTUM

State Rep. Cesar Blanco on Monday presented the team with an award for winning the 2015 National Junior High Championship. 'It's important to let kids know that they can rise to the top and be the best,' Blanco said. 'Oftentimes, we recognize a lot of the sports, and events like that, but chess is just as important. You have to use your mind to defeat your opponent, and these kids from El Paso demonstrated they are the best in the nation.'

"Blanco and EPISD leadership individually recognized the national champs for their big win before introducing all the students on the chess team –a team whose size has grown significantly in just three years. ...chess coach Saul Ramirez said, 'We started with a group of four kids. Last year we had 12, and now we have more than 60 students participating. I have had parents specifically bring their kids to Henderson so they have a chance to play at a national championship.'

"Initially Lirio Gomez was the only girl on the team, but through the exposure and accolades on campus emerged a new all girls team, comprised of 25 students."

– EPISD News

APPENDIX

AFTERWORD

I first heard the story of the Henderson Middle School Chess Team in 2016, while delivering staff development in El Paso, Texas. Both the teachers that day, as well as myself, were having a tough time getting started that morning, so I decided to do something a little differently. I asked the teachers in the room to share any success stories that they have recently experienced with their students.

As the teachers began to volunteer their stories, I saw what I thought was a tech/AV staff member working on a sound system near the stage. A participant, Sarah Aguirre, pointed to him and shouted, "Adrian has a story!"

It was at that moment that I first heard about the miracle of the Henderson Chess Team, straight from the mouth of Adrian Herrera. And I was astonished.

He told me that the majority of students were ELLs. That they came from one of the poorest zip codes in the United States. That they won the national championship. That their coach was a former chess champion himself. It was unbelievable.

For the rest of the day, I could not stop thinking about the story. I talked about it with anyone that would listen. "Have you heard about the Henderson Chess Team?!" I was amazed that day, how many people had NOT heard about their remarkable feats.

It was then, I realized, that I had been given a task. I needed to share the story of the Henderson Chess Team with everyone I knew. This had to be my next book. I needed their coach, Saul Ramirez, to share the story with me in detail.

To capture the story of Saul and the students, I went to El Paso with my good friend, M. Rutledge McCall, who had more experience than me in recording and narrating the stories of others. After gathering hours of interview coverage, we were ready to write.

This is how *The Champions' Game* came to life.

So many people helped in the creation of this book. Thank you especially to our wordsmiths: Melinda Base, Anna Matis, and Meg White; our editors: Dorothy Brady and Jenny White; and our talented graphic designer: Anne-Charlotte Patterson.

Above all, it has been amazing for all of us to hear and retell the stories of these 12 children. And I'm grateful to God to have been a part of it.

John Seidlitz

 **SAUL RAMIREZ** is the chess coach and art teacher at Henderson Middle School in El Paso, Texas, where he coached his students to win the national chess championships in 2015 and 2016. Ramirez grew up in El Paso's Segundo Barrio, located in one of the poorest zip codes in the United States. When he discovered chess as a child, it created a pathway out of misfortune. Ramirez, like his current students, competed and became a champion in various tournaments. Ramirez graduated from the University of Texas at El Paso (UTEP) in May 2010 and started teaching at Henderson Middle School in August of that same year, where he continues to create new paths for the dreams of his students. He lives in El Paso with his wife, Edna, and two children, Saul Jr. and Frida.

JOHN SEIDLITZ is an author and educator, who provides professional development for teachers of immigrant students. He is the co-author of the children's book *Sometimes*, which chronicles the story of elementary age Mexican immigrants. Seidlitz lives in Irving, Texas, with his wife and five children.